2014

Samsung

GALAXY S 5

The 100% Unofficial User Guide

By Aaron J. Halbert

Foreword

Thank you very much for purchasing *Samsung Galaxy S5: The 100% Unofficial User Guide*. I have worked hard to compile only the most relevant and useful information for you, and I firmly believe that you will get your money's worth. Better yet, when you are finished with this book, your skills and knowledge will put you among the top 1% of Galaxy S5 power users.

If you have any feedback on this book, please feel free to email me at AJH@AaronHalbert.com or post a review on Amazon. By doing so, you will be helping all S5 users get the information they need, and you will also have my enduring gratitude. I carefully read and consider all the comments I get, because I believe in listening to my customers.

Before we begin, a couple things:

First, throughout this book I sometimes suggest you purchase apps or accessories to improve your Galaxy S5 experience. I am NOT affiliated with any of these companies, nor do I receive any sort of compensation from them. All of my recommendations are based on my own experience and research and are completely independent. My opinion is not for sale.

Second, if you'd like to receive updates for this book as I release them, please sign up on my Galaxy S5 mailing list (p. 307). I will never share your email address with a third party.

Contents at a Glance

Detailed Contents

Chapter 1: Introduction

Thank you for purchasing *Samsung Galaxy S5: The 100% Unofficial User Guide*! This book is designed to help you unlock the potential of your S5 regardless of your previous Android experience. If you're brand new to Android, you will find that everything is explained from the ground up. If you already know your way around an Android device and are looking for S5-specific information, you can easily skip straight to the intermediate and advanced chapters.

Click any underlined text to jump to a new section of this book. External URLs (starting with http://) are links to websites rather than locations in this book. If you are reading this book on a tablet, phone, or computer, you can also click http:// links to open them in your web browser.

However, if you're using an e-ink Kindle device like the Paperwhite, your web browser won't be capable of opening most external links and you'll need to type the URL into your computer or other device.

To make this easier, I give you a short link (e.g., http://goo.gl/8Z3Uww) for long or complicated external URLs. These are much quicker to type and will take you to the same place.

Structure of the Book

In Chapter 2, About the Galaxy S5 (p. 15), I briefly recount the history of the Galaxy S series. I explain what's new in the Galaxy S5 and what has stayed the same.

Chapter 3, Getting Started (p. 17), guides you through initial setup and helps you get your S5 up and running.

Chapter 4, Fundamentals for New Users (p. 33), is a Galaxy S5 crash course for first-time Android users.

Chapters 5-7, Basic Functions (p. 72), Intermediate Functions – Useful Tips & Tricks (p. 182), and Advanced Functions (p. 251), are the core chapters of this book and cumulatively build your knowledge and skills with the Galaxy S5.

Chapter 8, <u>What Do These Apps Do?</u> (p. 273), provides brief explanations and reviews of the apps that come pre-loaded on the S5. In some cases, I suggest alternatives.

In Chapter 9, <u>The 50 All-Time Best Android Apps</u> (p. 280), I recommend my 50 most-used third-party apps (i.e., apps that do not come pre-loaded on the Galaxy S5). All of these apps are very high quality and will appeal to many different types of users. This chapter includes the entirety of my book, *The 50 All-Time Best Android Apps.*

Finally, in Chapter 10, <u>Accessory Shopping Guide</u> (p. 297), I review the types of accessories available for the Galaxy S5, provide examples, and make some recommendations.

Why Buy This Book?

Although it's possible to learn the Galaxy S5's features through online research and experimentation, it's a lot easier and faster to use this book. It consolidates everything you need to know in one place and presents the information in a logical and sequential fashion that you won't find anywhere else.

In this book, I will tell you how each and every app and feature works, but I won't stop there. I will also tell you which are worthwhile and which are gimmicks. I will suggest third-party alternatives that I trust. You will benefit from my years of experience with Android and other mobile platforms.

Other authors might assume that you already understand core concepts, which can lead to confusion and frustration. On the other hand, I make as few assumptions as possible and explain everything from the ground up. But, I believe all of my readers are smart and capable. I won't baby you; I will teach you.

I have organized this book so that you can read it cover-to-cover, or just open it to the page you need. It's full of hyperlinks, so you can easily jump around and find the information you're looking for.

Simply put, if you are a brand new Android user and you don't know the Play Store from the App Drawer, this book will teach you from first principles. If you already know and love Android, this book will teach you all the particular ins and outs of the Galaxy S5.

Who Am I?

Who am I, and what are my qualifications?

First, I am a power user and enthusiast. I have owned and used nearly 10 different Android devices since Android first hit the market in 2008 on the T-Mobile G1. I have pushed each one to its limits, both in stock and rooted configurations, and I have taught countless others to do the same. In the decade before Android hit the market, I used numerous Windows Mobile and Palm OS phones and PDAs. In fact, I got my first one in 2002. I have written for several enthusiast websites, including one popular one that I started, owned, and ran in the early 2000s. This ain't my first rodeo.

I am also the author of *Samsung Galaxy Note 3: The 100% Unofficial User Guide*, a bestselling and well-reviewed guide to the Note 3. Check it out on Amazon:

http://www.amazon.com/dp/1494832631/

The possibilities offered by the Galaxy S5 and other current Android phones are absolutely amazing. The first smartphones were little more than glorified day planners; today, the Galaxy S5 can do nearly any task that your home computer or laptop can do—if you know how to use it.

If you want to make the most of your Galaxy S5, read this guide.

Chapter 2: About the Galaxy S5

Design & Features

Today, Samsung is a huge name in the smartphone world. As of February 2014, it had 27% market share according to the market research firm comScore, second only to Apple (41.3%) and well ahead of third-place LG (6.8%). But it wasn't always this way. In fact, it wasn't until 2010 when Samsung released the Galaxy S series that it achieved real success in the smartphone market. Every year since then, Samsung has packed its best technology into one phone and released it as a new Galaxy S. In particular, the Galaxy S2 is considered to have set a new standard for design and performance of Android phones, catapulting Samsung to the top and paving the way for hundreds of millions of future Galaxy S sales. In this way, the Galaxy S5 is the latest entry in history's most successful line of Android phones. It's kind of a big deal.

In my opinion, the Galaxy S5 is more fresh and exciting than the S3 or S4 that many of you are upgrading from. Why? Samsung tried to distinguish the S3 and S4 by packing in as many features as possible, such as eye movement tracking, hand waving gestures, pedometers, and more. While interesting, those features gave the S3 and S4 a gimmicky feel. With the Galaxy S5, Samsung has gone back to basics. It has chosen a few areas in which to make the Galaxy S5 excel and really focused on them, leaving out the gimmicks. Let's talk about what separates the Galaxy S5 from the rest of the Android pack.

- **A Powered-Up Camera**: The Galaxy S5 sports a 16-megapixel rear camera that is capable of taking 4K (UHD) video as well as HDR photos and video with a real-time preview. (HDR means those super-saturated, high-color pictures that pop from the screen so well.) The Galaxy S5's camera is also capable of autofocusing in 0.3 seconds, so you'll get less blur than ever before. Additionally, there are modes in which the Galaxy S5 can refocus and apply effects even after you've taken a shot.

- **A Fingerprint Reader**: Apple's current flagship phone, the iPhone 5s, features a press-and-hold fingerprint reader for fast device unlocking and app purchase authorizations. Samsung is striking back with the Galaxy S5, which also has a built-in fingerprint reader, albeit one that works with a swiping action. In addition to phone locking and data security, the fingerprint reader can be used to authorize PayPal transactions, a feature completely unique to the S5.

- **Improved Fitness Tracking**: The mobile fitness market is growing, and Samsung has crosshairs on it. Previous Galaxy S and Galaxy Note smartphones included the S Health app, but Samsung has completely overhauled the app for the Galaxy S5 to make it more practical and useful. You can use S Health to track your calorie intake, steps, exercise, and weight more easily and efficiently than ever before. The Galaxy S5 also has a heart rate sensor built into the rear LED flash mechanism, which feeds cardio data to the S Health app. Additionally, the Galaxy S5 is waterproof and dustproof to the IP67 standard, which means that it can keep up with an active lifestyle.

- **A "Modern Glam" Look**: The Galaxy S5 is available in a variety of colors and features a new, leather-inspired back cover.

In addition to these features, the Galaxy S5 also has a wide variety of improvements such as Download Booster, which combines your 4G and Wi-Fi connections for super-fast downloads; a new and more streamlined user interface; Android 4.4 KitKat; a brand new superfast processor; a USB 3.0 port for faster charging and data transfer; a brighter screen; special power-saving modes; compatibility with Gear 2 and Gear Fit; and more.

Specifications

The table below shows the Galaxy S5's hardware specifications alongside those of the S3 and S4.

	S3	S4	S5
Size	136.6 x 70.6 x 8.6 mm	136.6 x 69.8 x 7.9 mm	142.0 x 72.5 x 8.1 mm
Weight	133g	130g	145g
Screen	4.8" HD Super AMOLED (1280x720)	5" Full HD Super AMOLED (1920 x 1080)	5.1" Full HD Super AMOLED (1920 x 1080)
Storage	16 / 32 / 64 GB + microSD	16 / 32 / 64 GB + microSD	16 / 32 GB + microSD
Processor	1.4 GHz Quad-Core	1.9 GHz Quad-Core	2.5 GHz Quad-Core
RAM	1 GB	2 GB	2 GB
Camera	8 MP / 1.9 MP front	13 MP / 2 MP front	16 MP / 2 MP front
Battery	2,100 mAh	2,600 mAh	2,800 mAh

Chapter 3: Getting Started

Galaxy S5 Anatomy

The photos below show the anatomy of the Galaxy S5.

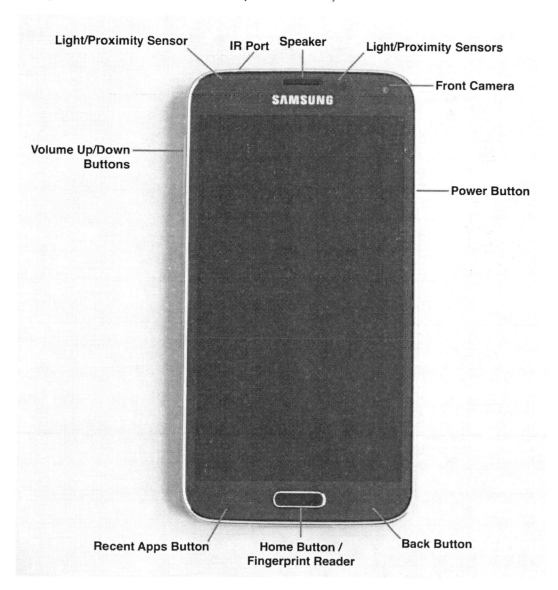

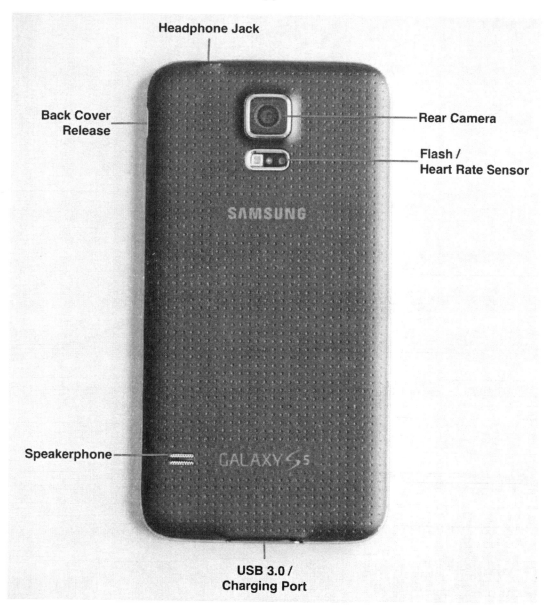

Headphone Jack

Back Cover
Release

Rear Camera

Flash /
Heart Rate Sensor

SAMSUNG

Speakerphone

GALAXY S 5

USB 3.0 /
Charging Port

Initial Hardware Setup

Before you can start using your Galaxy S5, you'll need to set it up for the first time. Remove your Galaxy S5's battery from its plastic baggie. There may also be a plastic film on the device's screen. If so, leave it on for now to protect the Galaxy S5 while you set it up.

Find a smooth surface and place the Galaxy S5 face down. Remove the back cover by placing your fingernail in the groove on the upper-right-hand side of the device, near the power button. ("Back Cover Release" in the image above.) The back cover should begin to pop up fairly easily, allowing you to work your finger around the edges and remove it completely. The plastic is flexible and will not break easily, but at the same time, you should not have to use a great deal of force. If you have trouble removing the back cover, make sure that you are starting from the correct groove.

After you have successfully removed the back cover, you will need to insert from 1 to 3 components. These include:

- **Battery**, which should come with a partial charge out of the box.

- **Micro SIM card**, if you are on a GSM network like T-Mobile or AT&T. Your Micro SIM card contains your account information and allows your Galaxy S5 to connect to your carrier's network. If you are a new customer of your carrier, your Micro SIM card may come pre-installed in the phone. If you are on Sprint or another CDMA network, your Galaxy S5 will neither need nor accept a SIM card, and instead you will need to call your carrier or take your Galaxy S5 into a retail location to activate it. Verizon, while technically a CDMA network like Sprint, is a unique case and does require a Micro SIM card for full data functionality.

- **Micro SD memory card**, if you have one. Whereas a SIM card stores your cellular account information, a Micro SD card stores data such as photos, apps, music, videos, and so on, and can be used regardless of your carrier. Because the Galaxy S5 has a large built-in storage capacity (16 GB on the base model), a Micro SD card is less of a necessity now than it was a few years ago, when phones had 1 GB or less of built-in storage. Nevertheless, Micro SD cards are inexpensive (less than $1/GB) and are extremely useful if you plan to store a lot of media on your Galaxy S5 or if you want to store backups of your data. See Chapter 10, Accessory Shopping Guide (p. 297), for more information.

The photo below demonstrates the correct way to insert your Micro SIM and Micro SD cards. Your Micro SIM goes in the lower, larger slot, and your Micro SD card—if you have one—goes in the upper, smaller slot. Both will firmly click into place.

Now, you can remove the protective plastic film on the Galaxy S5's screen. Note that there is also a very thin and hard to see plastic film over the camera's lens, so make sure you remove it, too!

Initial Software Setup

After you have completed this process and firmly snapped the back cover into place, you can plug it in using the supplied power adapter and cable. An orange-red LED light in the front upper-left-hand corner of the Galaxy S5 will illuminate to indicate the device is charging. Turn the Galaxy S5 on by pressing and holding the power button on the upper-right-hand edge of the device. After the device powers up for the first time, you will see the screen pictured below. On this screen, select your preferred language. Tap "Accessibility" if you are hard of seeing or hearing to set up some features like text vocalization and screen magnification. Then, tap "Start" to proceed to the Wi-Fi configuration screen.

Note that some of the following steps may happen out of order on your Galaxy S5. The order can change depending on the information you provide throughout the setup process. Don't be alarmed—you'll get to everything eventually.

If you have a Wi-Fi connection available, first tap the On-Off button in the upper-right-hand corner of the screen to power on your Wi-Fi chip. Your Galaxy S5 will search for available Wi-Fi networks and display them in a list, as shown below. If your carrier supports Wi-Fi calling, you may also see a pop-up notification pertaining to that. If so, click "Learn More" and tap through the dialog boxes

Smart network switch is a feature that automatically switches your Galaxy S5 from Wi-Fi to cellular data if it detects your Wi-Fi signal is getting weak (for example, if you get too far away from your wireless router). However, I suggest leaving it off. Android's default network management does a very good job of choosing the right network even without this "feature" enabled.

Once you see your preferred network, tap on it. You will be prompted to enter your network's WEP/WPA password. Do so and tap "Connect." You will see a dialog box that says "Wi-Fi Connected." Tap "OK" and then "Next." If you do not see this dialog box and your Galaxy S5 says "Saved/Secured" under the name of your network, then you have not successfully connected. Tap the network name, "Forget," and then re-enter your password to try again.

If you do *not* have a Wi-Fi connection available, simply tap "Next" and the phone will use your carrier's wireless data connection instead, although it may take several minutes for your device to connect to the cellular network for the first time. Note that this may cost you money or use up your data quota, depending on how your phone's data plan is configured with your carrier. I recommend using Wi-Fi when possible.

If you try to proceed without connecting to Wi-Fi, but your Galaxy S5 keeps pestering you to connect, it's because it doesn't have a cellular data connection yet. Give it a few minutes before proceeding, or move elsewhere if you're in an area with poor cell coverage. You will be able to proceed without a Wi-Fi connection once a cellular connection has been established.

Next, you will be prompted to accept Samsung's EULA (End User Licensing Agreement) and consent to provide diagnostic and usage data. You must accept the EULA to continue. The diagnostic and usage agreement allows Samsung to collect anonymous data to find and squash software bugs. I usually leave it enabled. It won't impact your privacy or battery life.

At some point during the setup process, you will be prompted to enable Google's app verification procedure. You will definitely want to tap "Accept." Verify Apps is an official Google feature that runs in the background and protects your Galaxy S5 from harmful and invasive applications. If a problem app is detected, you will be notified and prompted to remove it. Sometimes, this prompt does not appear until you have completely finished initial software setup.

Next, you will be prompted to log in to your Google account, or create one if you do not already have one. If you use Gmail, you have one, so tap "Yes."

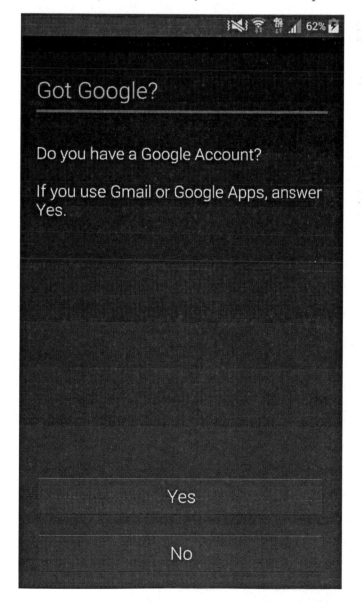

If you do not have one, tap "No" to create a new one for free. I cannot stress the importance of this enough. Android is a Google product and most of its features rely on you having a Google account. If you do not, you will miss out on many crucial features of your Galaxy S5. For example, without a Google Account you will not be able to use the built-in Gmail app, you will not be able to sync and backup your contacts, you will not be able to sync your bookmarks and passwords through Chrome, and you will not be able to download any new apps from the Google Play Store.

You may also be prompted to set up Google Plus and/or Google Wallet. What are they? Google Plus is a social networking website—Google's competitor to Facebook. Feel free to create a free account if you want to try connecting with friends, family, or coworkers on Google Plus. Google Wallet, on the other hand, allows you to set up a credit or debit card to use in the Google Play store. If you plan to buy apps, music, video, or books from Google, go ahead and set up a card through Google Wallet. It is safe to do so.

Next, you will be asked whether you want to "Back up data to your Google Account." I recommend enabling this feature. It will ensure your contacts, email, calendars, and some other data such as Google Talk chat logs are automatically backed up to Google's servers. This feature does not back up everything on your Galaxy S5—only what I just mentioned—but is nonetheless very useful. With this feature, if your phone is lost or stolen, your critical data will automatically be restored to your replacement phone upon logging in to your Google Account.

You will also be asked to configure your location settings. Personally, I leave all the boxes checked and grant my phone and apps full access to my location to get the most out of my Galaxy S5. In my judgment, enabling location settings is not a pressing threat to privacy. Google and other app developers are interested in gathering your location data to serve you with better information and improve their own products, not to meddle in your personal affairs. My advice? Leave your location settings enabled and enjoy the benefits, like improved local searches, Google Now (p. 166) customization, and more. If you are very concerned about your privacy, it is your decision to disable location services, but be aware that apps like Google Maps won't work right.

After you have gotten through all of that, you will be prompted to enter your name, as shown below. Enter it and tap the right-facing arrow to continue.

Next, you will be presented with a chance to create a Samsung account, which provides various services and enhancements to Samsung applications included on your phone. To do so, tap "Create new account" and fill in your e-mail address, password, date of birth, and other information. The process is optional. Personally, I do not use a Samsung account, because a Google account already does nearly everything a Samsung account does, and a Samsung account requires additional, battery-draining account syncing. (The most significant benefits of a Samsung account are text message and photo backup, but you can better accomplish those things using SMS Backup & Restore (p. 291) and Dropbox, respectively.) My verdict? Skip the Samsung account.

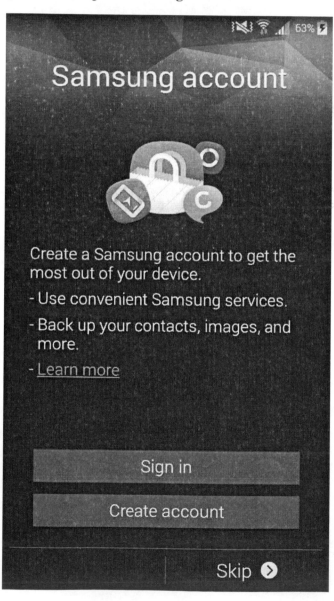

Next, you will have a chance to sign into your Dropbox account or create a new account if you do not have one. Dropbox is a cloud storage service that allows you to store files on Dropbox's servers and access them from anywhere you have an Internet connection, including your Galaxy S5, your desktop or laptop PC, your tablet if you have one, or even a web browser on a public computer. Dropbox makes your files available anywhere you go.

In my opinion, Dropbox is a fantastic service. I store all of my work files and documents in my Dropbox, which allows me to access them from anywhere at any time—including from my Galaxy S5—flexibility that serves me well when I am away from my home office.

As if these features aren't enough, Dropbox also stores every single version of the files you save in it, meaning that if you ever want to revert back to an old version of a document, you can easily do so. Because of this feature, you never have to worry about losing your data or incorrectly overwriting a file. Additionally, because Samsung has partnered with Dropbox, you receive 50 GB free for two years when you sign in using your Galaxy S5—25 times the amount of storage given to normal Dropbox users. Take advantage of this opportunity and I promise you won't regret it.

Finally, you will be given a chance to name your Galaxy S5.

Enter whatever you like and click "Finish" to star using your Galaxy S5. (Don't use a name that's too weird, though, since other people on your networks will be able to see it!)

Skip the "Easy Mode" checkbox—with this book, you don't need no stinkin' Easy Mode. Your device will work for a few moments and then bring you to a screen like this: the home screen. Congratulations—almost done!

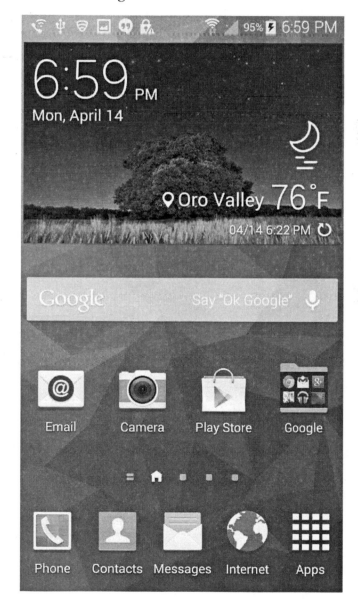

The final step is to configure your voicemail inbox. This is usually only necessary if you're a new customer to your carrier. To do so, tap the Phone app and then the "Keypad" tab. Tap the cassette tape icon below the star ("*") key and follow the voice prompts to set up your inbox for the first time.

I also suggest you do two other things relatively soon after you get your Galaxy S5: set up a lock screen and device tracking features. If your phone is lost or stolen, these features will help you protect your data, and ideally, recover your phone. Read about the lock screen here (p. 60) and here (p. 187), and read setup instructions for device location features here (p. 189).

Chapter 4: Fundamentals for New Users

Welcome to Android! More specifically, welcome to TouchWiz, Samsung's own version of the Android user interface.

TouchWhat? Let me explain.

You probably know that Google makes the Android OS. Android is an operating system similar to Microsoft Windows or Mac OSX, but it's designed for smartphones and tablets instead of desktops and laptops. However, Google's "pure" form of Android is actually only sold on a few select devices such as Google's own Nexus series. Most Android devices sold today come from third-party companies that put their own software "layer" on top of the Android operating system. (That's a totally different product philosophy than Apple. Apple makes 100% of the iPhones and iPads in the world, and they all run exactly the same operating system.)

TouchWiz is the layer that Samsung puts on top of Google's "pure" form of the Android OS. TouchWiz isn't just an app, though—it's a collection of apps, tweaks, features, and graphic designs. It refers to the entirety of the changes that Samsung makes to the Android OS to make it a unique Samsung experience.

Some of the elements of TouchWiz include:

- A custom home screen and app drawer;

- A custom system settings menu;

- Samsung apps like S Health;

- A better camera app;

- A smattering of special features like Multi Window (p. 182);

- And more.

Think of it this way: An HP computer runs the Windows OS, but comes pre-loaded with HP-specific software layered on top of Windows so you know you've got an HP. TouchWiz refers to all of the Samsung-specific software that it layers on top of Android.

Here is an example of the TouchWiz home screen (first image) compared to the pure Android home screen (second image):

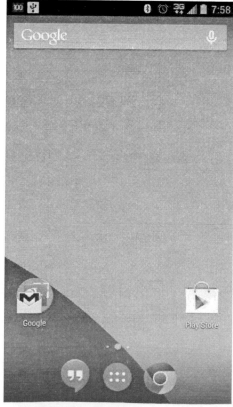

Different, but not *that* different, right? Right. TouchWiz is the same old Android, just more dressed up.

Components of the User Interface

You can think about TouchWiz in five main parts:

- **The Home Screen(s)**

- **The Notification Panel**

- **The Lock Screen**

- **The App Drawer**

- **System Settings**

Almost everything you do on your Galaxy S5 will take place in one of these areas, or in an app. You can think of apps as your destinations, and these parts of TouchWiz as the roads that get you to your destinations. In this chapter, I will teach you everything there is to know about these areas of TouchWiz.

First, though, let's briefly talk about the physical controls on the Galaxy S5. You need to understand these before you can efficiently use your device.

> When the Galaxy S5 starts up or when you unplug the charger, it will show a warning to make sure the back cover and/or the charging port cover is closed. This is automatic and does not mean that either cover is necessarily open—it's just a precautionary warning so that your Galaxy S5 lives up to its promised water resistance capabilities.

Physical Controls – For the most basic operations

The Power Button (power on/off, reboot, airplane mode, & emergency mode)

A single press of the power button wakes the Galaxy S5 or puts it to sleep. I use the terms "wake" and "sleep" instead of "on" and "off" because the Galaxy S5 is actually powered on even when it is asleep—it has to be, in order to receive calls and other communications.

On the other hand, a long press of the power button brings up the following options:

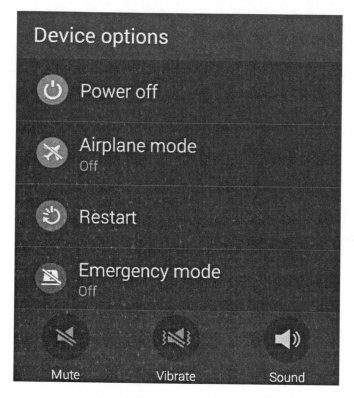

- **Power off**: Turn off the device completely. This is different than putting it to sleep with a single press of the power button. When you power it off, it will no longer send or receive any communications, and the screen will be completely shut off. To use the Galaxy S5 again, turn it on with another long press of the power button.

- **Airplane mode**: Leave the device powered on, but turn off all wireless communications, including cellular, Wi-Fi, Bluetooth, NFC, and so on. Although use of electronic devices is now permitted from boarding to de-boarding on all U.S. airlines, you are still required to turn off all wireless functions during takeoff and landing. Airplane mode comes in handy for this.

- **Restart**: Reboot your Galaxy S5. Useful if it's exhibiting unusual or sluggish behavior. In fact, I recommend rebooting your Galaxy S5 at least once every few days to keep it operating at its best.

- **Emergency mode**: Enable a safety and power conservation mode. Emergency mode gives you big buttons on your home screen to easily share your location or use your camera's flash as a flashlight. Emergency mode also makes your battery last as long as possible by minimizing screen brightness, displaying only black and white, and slowing down the Galaxy S5's CPU.

Useful if you're in a bad situation, if your battery is dying, or both. Emergency mode is a new feature not previously seen on any Samsung device.

- **Mute, Vibrate, and Sound**: The options "Mute," "Vibrate," and "Sound" are mutually exclusive, meaning that only one can be selected at a time. "Mute" will prevent your Galaxy S5 from making any noises or vibrating. "Vibrate" will permit it to vibrate, but not to make any noises using the speaker. "Sound" will allow it to vibrate as well as play sounds such as alerts and ringtones.

Volume Up/Down Buttons (adjust volume, vibrate & silent modes)

The Galaxy S5 has five separate volume settings: Ringtone, Media, Notifications, System, and In-Call volume. I know this sounds complicated, but in practice, you only have to remember one rule: the Volume Up and Volume Down buttons generally control what you want them to control, when you want it.

For example, if you're playing a game, they'll control the game's sound volume. If you're in a call, they'll control the speaker volume. Easy, right? But if you want the slightly more complicated explanation, read on.

Here is what each volume setting controls, specifically:

- **Ringtone Volume**: The volume of the ringtone that plays when you receive a phone call.

- **Media Volume**: The volume of audio that plays in music apps, video apps, games, etc.

- **Notification Volume**: The volume of audio alerts that play upon receiving emails, text messages, and so on.

- **System Volume**: The volume of audio for the phone keypad tone, touch sounds, key presses, and so on.

- **In-Call Volume**: The volume of the speaker when you're in a voice call.

The Volume Up and Volume Down buttons only ever directly control Ringtone, Media, and In-Call volumes. Let me repeat that: the Volume buttons only ever directly adjust the Ringtone, Media, or In-Call volume levels, not the notification or system volume levels. The settings they control depend on what the Galaxy S5 is doing at the time you press them. If the Galaxy S5 is on a system screen such as a home screen or the app drawer, the buttons will adjust the Ringtone volume. If it is playing a movie or a game, the buttons will adjust the Media volume. If you are in a call, the buttons will adjust the In-Call volume.

You can hold Volume Up or Volume Down to rapidly increase or decrease the Ringtone or Media volume, but note that when holding Volume Down, the volume slider will pause at vibrate mode, which is still one notch above the mute setting. You must release the Volume Down button and press it one more time to fully mute the Galaxy S5. (You can also mute the Galaxy S5 by holding the power button and tapping "Mute" on the menu that appears.)

Also, remember that I said the Volume buttons never *directly* control Notification and System volume? The exception is that they *indirectly* control Notification and System volume if you fully mute the Galaxy S5. When the Ringtone volume is muted this way, Notification and System volumes are also temporarily muted. However, the Media volume is not muted. So, how do you specifically adjust the Notification and System volume levels, since the buttons don't control them? Anytime you press Volume Up or Volume Down, you can tap the gear icon that appears on the screen to manually adjust these volume levels on the Galaxy S5, as shown below.

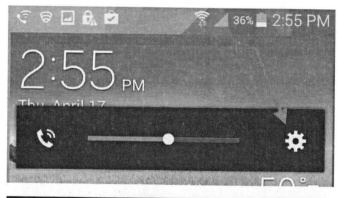

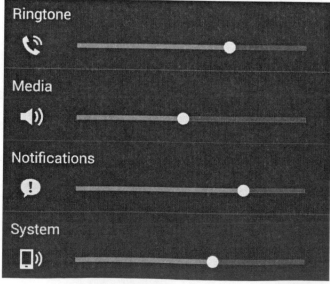

As you can see, In-Call volume cannot be adjusted from this menu. It can only be adjusted while a voice call is active.

Home Button (launch home screen, quickly issue voice commands)

The physical button centered below the Galaxy S5's screen is the home button. Tapping it once will take you back to the home screen from any other screen. You can also quickly double-tap the home button to open S Voice (p. 180), or tap and hold it to open Google Now (p. 166), two different voice command systems that I will discuss in more depth later. The home button also doubles as the Galaxy S5's fingerprint scanner.

Recent and Back Buttons (switch/quit apps, open the menu, return to last screen)

The recent and back buttons are soft buttons (i.e., non-click buttons) to the left and right of the home button, respectively, and are only easily visible when backlit. Tapping the recent button brings up a list of all of your recently used apps. From here, swipe up and down to scroll through the list. Tapping on one of these apps will open it; you can also close apps and free memory by swiping them left or right. I almost never do this, though; with 2GB of memory, the Galaxy S5 almost never slows down due to a lack of RAM.

There are two buttons at the bottom of this screen. The left button opens a system settings page that shows memory usage. The right button closes all active apps.

The back button, on the other hand, usually works like a back button in a web browser, taking you to the last screen you were on. However, it sometimes does other things like hiding the on-screen keyboard. The best way to get the hang of the back button is just to try it.

If you have owned an Android device in the past, you may be wondering where the menu button is. The answer is that it's gone, completely replaced by the recent button. In Android 4.4 KitKat, Google ditched the dedicated menu button in favor of the three-dot, on-screen menu button which looks like this:

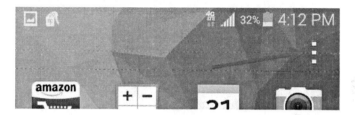

So, any time that you would have reached for your menu button, look for those three vertical dots instead.

> You can also long-press the recent button to simulate the menu button. This is a helpful, but undocumented trick!

The Home Screen – Where the action starts

Now that you are familiar with the basic controls of the Galaxy S5, we can start to discuss its software. If you still have this screen pulled up on your Galaxy S5, then you are on the home screen.

If you don't see this screen, just press the home button! Note that your home screen may look slightly different depending on which carrier you have and whether you have already customized your Galaxy S5. The above screenshot shows the default home screen configuration.

What Is the Home Screen?

The home screen is where everything starts on Android; you might compare it to the desktop of your home or laptop computer. However, unlike on a PC, none of the icons you'll see on the Android home screen are files. Instead, they are all app shortcuts. You may be used to saving files on the desktop of your PC, but that is not possible on Android. Files can only be accessed from within apps. Another difference is that there are actually multiple home screens on Android. From the above screen, try swiping left and right. You will see **secondary, adjacent home screens** with other app shortcuts and widgets. (If you swipe all the way to the left, you will also bring up My Magazine (p. 274), a news and social media aggregator. My Magazine is really an app, though, not a part of the home screen.)

What exactly are widgets? They are mini-apps that you place directly on your home screen. Unlike full apps, which typically have a lot of features and options, widgets are usually designed to do only one or two high-priority things.

For example, as shown in the previous screenshot, the home screen has two widgets. The first one feeds you weather information and the second allows you to search Google using voice commands. In other words, they give you easier access to things that you might want to do on a regular basis, so you don't have to tap through to an app every time. That's the beauty of widgets.

Components of the Home Screen

There are many things happening on the home screen, so let's analyze them from top to bottom. In the following image, I have outlined the six major parts of the default home screen.

1. The horizontal bar at the very top of the screen is called the **status bar**. From right to left are the current time, the battery/charging indicator, the cell signal strength indicator, and the Wi-Fi signal strength indicator. The icons on the left are all notifications. Don't worry about these yet—I will explain them in more detail later in this section.

2. Below the status bar is a large **widget** containing the current time, date, and local weather conditions. Widgets can be nearly any size and contain a variety of different content. In essence, they are mini "apps" that you can place on your home screen for easy, bite-size functionality and information.

3. The Google box below the time/weather widget is yet another widget, and allows you to quickly perform a Google voice search.

4. Below the two widgets is a row of **app shortcuts**, including Email, Camera, Play Store, and a folder full of Google apps. These are not widgets; rather, they are shortcuts to full apps. Samsung has placed these four shortcuts on the home screen by default, but I will show you how to customize them shortly.

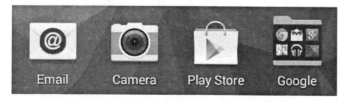

5. The next element is the row of symbols that includes a tiny house. In this screenshot, the house is highlighted in white, indicating that the device is currently showing the main home screen. Each of the squares represents **adjacent, secondary home screens**. You can switch to these secondary home screens by swiping left or right. The "equals sign" icon to the left of the house is <u>My Magazine</u> (p. 274), a news and social media aggregator app.

Below is an example of an adjacent home screen. It's not fundamentally different than the main home screen; it just provides additional space for app shortcuts and widgets.

From nearly any screen on your Galaxy S5, press the home button to return to the last home screen you were viewing. If it was a secondary, adjacent home screen, press the home button again to return to the main home screen.

6. The bottommost element of the home screen is the **app tray**. The app tray is a special place for you to place your four most important app shortcuts, and unlike other app shortcuts, these stay visible on all home screens. By default, the Galaxy S5 app tray contains Phone, Contacts, Messages, Internet, and Apps (a special shortcut to the app drawer that you can't remove).

As you may have noticed, the shortcuts in the app tray stay the same regardless of which home screen is selected, unlike the app shortcuts on the home screens themselves. This is why the app tray is a great place to put your most-used apps.

Editing Existing Shortcuts and Widgets

The strength of the home screen is its customizability, so let's talk about how to make your home screen your own. We'll start with the default configuration:

Let's say I want to rearrange the Email, Camera, Play Store, and Google shortcuts. Normally, the way to do this is to tap and hold on the shortcuts one at a time, and drag them to their new location.

However, there's a bit of a problem if I want to keep the Camera shortcut on this home screen—there's nowhere else to place it! I need to free up some room first. So, instead, I will tap and hold the large date/time/weather widget, drag it up to the "Remove" bar that appears, and release it.

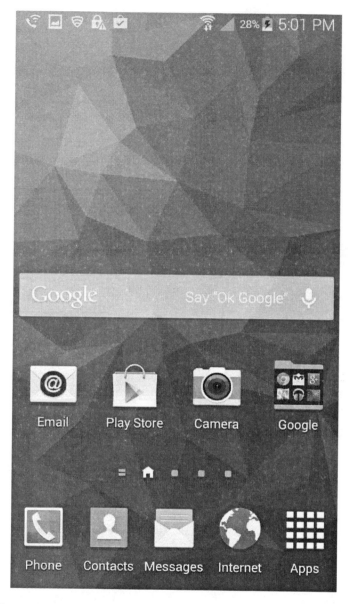

This is much better. Now, I can do some rearranging as I originally planned. I will tap and hold each of these shortcuts for approximately a second, and then move them to their desired place.

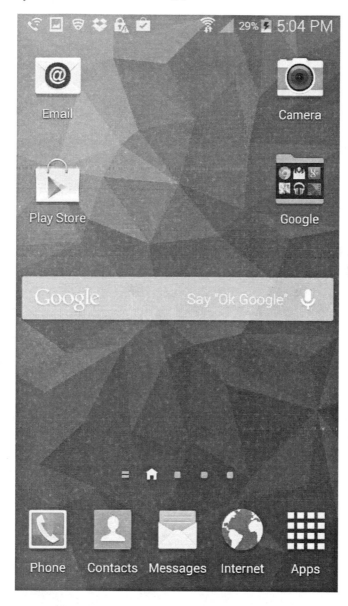

By tapping, holding, and dragging, I have rearranged the row of app shortcuts as shown.

> You can manipulate app shortcuts in the app tray at the bottom of the screen in almost exactly the same way—just tap and hold.

It is also possible to move app shortcuts and widgets to adjacent home screens by tapping, dragging, and holding them against the left or right edge of the screen.

Adding Widgets, Changing Wallpaper, & Managing Adjacent Home Screens

To add widgets, change your background image, or edit/add/delete adjacent home screens, you need to pull up the home screen menu. Do so by tapping and holding the recent button, the non-click soft button to the left of the physical "home" key. Or, tap and hold on any blank home screen space.

You can do several different things from this menu:

- **Add, rearrange or remove home screens**: Swipe left and right to view and edit your currently active home screens. To remove a home screen and all of its app shortcuts and widgets, tap and hold until you feel a vibration, drag it to the "Remove" icon, and release. To rearrange home screens, tap, hold, and drag them to the left or right sides of the screen. To add a new home screen, swipe all the way to the right and tap the plus (+) sign. You can have a maximum of six secondary home screens.

- **Change wallpaper**: Your wallpaper is the background image of the home screen and/or lock screen (p. 60). Tap the "Wallpapers" icon to select from a variety of other preloaded options, or to use a photo taken with your Galaxy S5's camera. (To do the latter, after you've tapped "Wallpapers," tap the "More images" button in the lower-left-hand corner of the screen, then "Gallery," then "Just once.") Note that using darker wallpaper will increase your battery life.

- **Add widgets**: To view all of the widgets available on your Galaxy S5 and optionally add them to your home screens, tap the "Widgets" button. From this screen, you can swipe left and right to view all of your widgets. Once you've found a widget you want to place on one of your home screens, tap and hold until you feel a vibration. Drag and hold your finger over the far left or right side of the screen to switch between home screens. When you've found a place for your widget, release your finger.

- **Change the scroll effect and/or disable My Magazine:** Tap the "Home screen settings" button to access two settings: the transition effect when you swipe between home screens, and an option to remove My Magazine from the home screen.

> We haven't yet covered how to add new app shortcuts to the home screen. Keep reading—it's coming up in the section about the app drawer (p. 62).

The Notification Panel – Quickly change settings & get important info

Congratulations—you have now learned almost everything there is to know about home screens on TouchWiz. Now, I will discuss the notification panel, which is another very important component of the Galaxy S5's user interface. Place your finger on the status bar—the bar at the very top of your Galaxy S5's screen containing the time—and swipe down. You will reveal a screen like this:

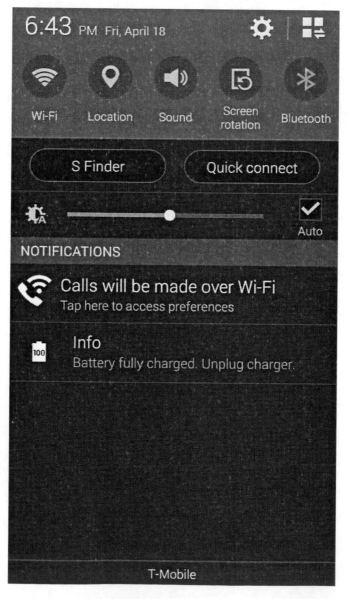

This is called the notification panel. Whereas the home screen(s) are dedicated to widgets and shortcuts for apps, the notification panel is a place where your Galaxy S5 reports important status information and provides quick access to some commonly used settings. Let's talk about what's going on in the notification panel, the same way we did for the home screen.

Components of the Notification Panel

At the top of the screen are the current time and date as well as two buttons—a gear and a symbol made up of several squares. Tapping the gear will take you to system settings (p. 68), which is the same as accessing the "Settings" app in the app drawer (p. 62).

The icon to the right of the gear is related to the next element in the notification panel—the group of toggle buttons including Wi-Fi, Location, Sound, Screen Rotation, and Bluetooth. Each of these buttons is called a toggle button, because it either switches a simple setting on or off, or rotates through a group of settings. For example, the Wi-Fi toggle button turns your Wi-Fi connection on or off. The Sound toggle button changes your sound settings from "Sound" (all sounds on), to "Vibrate" (sounds off; vibration on), to "Mute" (all sounds and vibration off). The icon to the right of the gear expands the number of toggle settings available.

You can also accomplish this quickly by dragging the notification panel down with two fingers instead of one.

You can adjust the arrangement of these toggle buttons by going to system settings → Notification Panel.

You can also swipe the main group of toggle buttons left and right to gain access to the second row of toggle buttons from the expanded view. For example, here I have swiped the toggle buttons partway to the left:

Unfortunately, however, this swiping action will not access any of the additional toggle buttons in the third or fourth row of the expanded view.

> You can also tap and hold on any of these notification toggles to open their corresponding settings page.

Below the group of toggle buttons are the S Finder (p. 222) and Quick Connect (p. 221) buttons and the screen brightness selector. If you check the "Auto" box, your Galaxy S5 will automatically adjust the brightness of the screen by measuring the light level of your surroundings. However, you can also control the brightness manually by moving the slider, and doing so will disable the "Auto" function if it is enabled.

Below the screen brightness selector is the main notification area. In this area, you will find notifications from apps or from the Android OS itself.

Working with Notifications

Notifications are the main way that apps communicate with you while you are not actively using them. They are very important because they enable your Galaxy S5 to perform valuable services in the background without your attention. For example, by default your Galaxy S5's Messages app will create a notification every time you receive a text message. Other apps, like stock tickers, can send you alerts whenever required, such as when a stock hits a target price. In the following screenshot, I have received a notification telling me about a text message from my friend Mike:

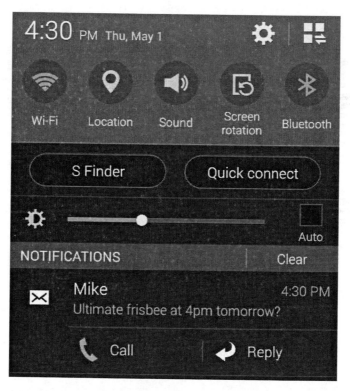

Most notifications do something when you tap on them; for example, tapping on this text message notification will open the Messages app and create a reply to Mike. Another example is the notification you receive after installing a new app from the Google Play Store, which, when tapped, will open the installed app. Notifications generally disappear ("are dismissed") after you tap them.

You can also hit the "Clear" button to dismiss all notifications without tapping them and triggering their actions. For example, hitting "Clear" on the screen above would dismiss the text message notification without opening the Messages app. To clear a single notification without tapping it, swipe it left or right.

You can expand some notifications by placing two fingers on them and dragging down. For example, you can do this with Gmail notifications to bring up Archive and Reply buttons in the notification panel itself.

Another thing to know is that some apps will create persistent notifications, some of which have special functions built into them. For example, in the screenshot above, my carrier offers an option to make all phone calls via Wi-Fi when possible. In this case, hitting "Clear" will not remove that notification. I also use some third-party MP3 player apps that create persistent notifications with back, forward, and pause buttons.

That's everything you need to know about the notification panel. You will find it's a very important part of your user experience. To close the notification panel, either swipe up from the bottom of the screen or tap the "Back" button.

The Lock Screen – Protect your personal information

The security risk involved in owning an Android smartphone is higher than ever before because they contain so much more sensitive data than 'dumb' phones. In the past, cellphones contained only your phone book and perhaps some text messages; today, they most likely contain your e-mail, photos, your banking information, your passwords, and so on. The lock screen is the main security mechanism to protect your data. When active, the lock screen prevents your Galaxy S5 from being used unless you provide the appropriate authentication. Typically, the lock screen will be activated every time the Galaxy S5 goes to sleep, so that a password is required every time it is woken up. The screenshot below shows the lock screen with the PIN function enabled:

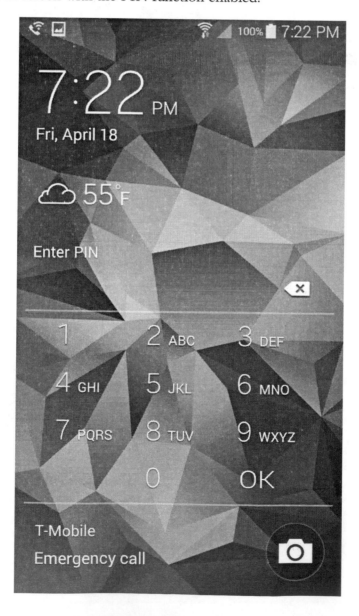

Instead of a PIN, it's also possible to use fingerprint recognition, pattern recognition, or a password. For example, the screenshot below shows pattern recognition in action:

It's also possible to disable the lock screen entirely or to use a zero-security, swipe-to-unlock option, but if you value your personal information at all, I don't suggest using these options.

You will learn how to <u>set up your lock screen and apply other security measures</u> (p. 187) shortly. For now, I just want you to understand what it's for and how it works.

The App Drawer – View all apps, delete apps, & create app shortcuts

The last major part of the TouchWiz interface is the app drawer. It contains all of the apps installed on your Galaxy S5, including the ones installed on your Galaxy S5 by default, as well as any third-party apps you have installed.

To open the app drawer, click the "Apps" shortcut in the app tray:

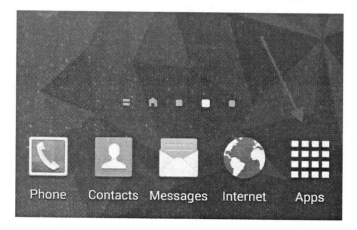

Upon doing so, you will be greeted by a screen like this:

This is the app drawer, which contains shortcuts to *all* of the apps installed on your Galaxy S5. It stands in contrast to the home screens, where you individually place only the shortcuts (and widgets) you want. In other words, the app drawer is a more complete, but less convenient way of accessing your apps.

By now, many of these elements will look familiar to you. At the top of the screen is the same status bar that is present on the home screen, and you can still swipe it down to reveal the notification panel. The lion's share of the screen is covered by app shortcuts, which upon being tapped will launch apps, just as they do on the home screen. At the bottom of the screen are a few small squares, one of which is highlighted. Similar to the home screen, this means you can swipe left and right to access additional screens. There is, however, no 'main' screen in the app drawer like there is with the home screens.

That said, there is at least one new element here: the three dots in the upper-right-hand corner of the screen, which brings up the app drawer menu. This menu contains a lot of important commands.

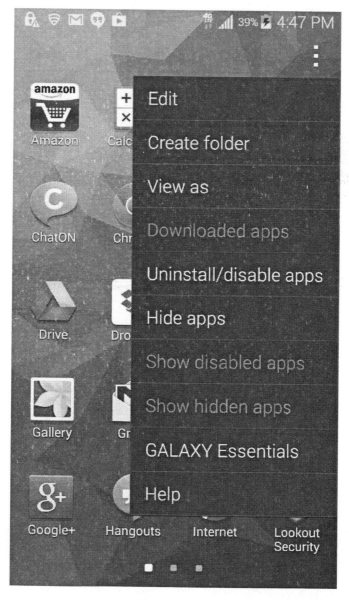

- **Edit**: The Edit option allows you to (1) rearrange apps in your app drawer, (2) create new pages for apps, (3) create new folders to organize your app shortcuts, (4) see information about apps, and (5) delete or disable apps. To use these features, enter Edit mode, tap and hold on an app shortcut, and then drag and release it over the appropriate option at the top of the screen.

Note that to rearrange apps in a non-alphabetical order, you must first go to the "View as" menu and change the mode to Custom.

- **Create folder**: Creates an empty folder, prompts you to name it, and allows you to specify which apps should go in it. This is the same option as the "create folder" option under the Edit menu.

- **View as**: Choose whether your apps are always sorted in alphabetical order. If you choose "Custom," use the Edit menu to rearrange them.

- **Downloaded apps**: If you have downloaded additional apps from the Google Play Store or other sources, this option will filter your apps and show only your downloaded apps.

- **Uninstall/disable apps**: From here, you can completely uninstall downloaded apps or disable non-essential apps that come preloaded on the Galaxy S5. Samsung does not allow you to completely uninstall any preloaded apps, but disabling them will freeze them and not allow them to run at all. I recommend disabling any built-in apps you do not use, because it will free up memory on your Galaxy S5, improve system performance, and increase battery life. In particular, feel free to disable carrier "bloatware"—useless apps that come preloaded on your Galaxy S5 that you'll never use.

- **Hide apps**: If there are any apps you do not wish to uninstall/disable or cannot uninstall disable, you can use this option to hide their icons from the app drawer.

- **Show disabled apps**: If you have disabled any apps, you can use this option to view and re-enable them.

- **Show hidden apps**: If you have hidden any apps, you can use this option to view and unhide them.

- **Galaxy Essentials**: This will show you a selection of Samsung apps that you can download to your Galaxy S5, such as the Samsung Gear Manager, the Samsung WatchON remote control app, a video editor, and more.

- **Help**: This screen contains several short tutorials about how to use the Galaxy S5's home screen and app drawer. All of the information in these tutorials is included in this book, but I recommend checking out these tutorials as a supplement.

Adding New App Shortcuts to Your Home Screen

When you tap and hold on an app shortcut in the app drawer, the Galaxy S5 will display a silhouette of your home screens, and give you a chance to copy the shortcut to one of your home screens or the app tray, if it has a free slot. (If it doesn't, go to the home screen, tap and hold an app shortcut in the app tray, and remove it to free up a space.)

Below, I have tapped and held the S Health app in the app drawer, and the Galaxy S5 is directing me to place a shortcut on one of my home screens.

If I had wanted to place the shortcut on an adjacent home screen, I would have dragged the shortcut to the far left or right edge of the screen, held it until the home screen switched over, and then released it.

As you may recall, this action is different than when you tap and hold an app shortcut on one of your home screens—in that case, you are given a chance to move the shortcut around on your home screens, remove it altogether, or place it into a folder.

To summarize, tapping and holding apps in the app drawer allows you to create a new shortcut on your home screen or in the app tray. Tapping and holding on an app shortcut that is already on your home screen allows you to modify a shortcut that has already been created. The app drawer is for comprehensive access to your apps; home screens are for your most-used apps and widgets.

System Settings – Customize Your Galaxy S5

Finally, you need to be familiar with the system settings screen on the Galaxy S5, because I will refer to it many times throughout this book. The system settings screen is the central control panel for your Galaxy S5, and includes settings for sound, the display, wireless connections, power conservation, and much, much more.

You can access system settings in two ways. First, you can tap the "Settings" icon in your app drawer:

Second, you can swipe down the notification panel and tap the gear icon in the upper-right-hand corner of the screen:

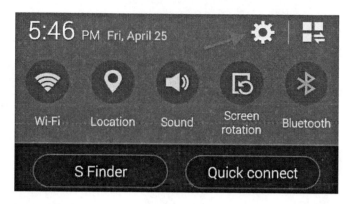

Transferring Your Data from Another Phone

By now, you should be getting more comfortable with your Galaxy S5. You've seen all of the major parts of the user interface and you should be getting a sense of how they all work together. But there's another important topic to cover— what's the best way to transfer your information from your previous phone?

From a Dumb Phone

If the Galaxy S5 is your first smartphone and your last phone was a "dumb" phone, there's good and bad news. The good news is that you won't have much information to transfer—probably just phone numbers. The bad news is that as dumb phones are becoming less common, data transfer programs are becoming less common. Your luck will depend on what make and model your last phone was.

And because there are hundreds, if not thousands of dumb phone models in existence, I can't offer you a one-size-fits-all solution. However, I can offer you some general advice. Here are the steps you should take to get your contacts from your dumb phone to your S5:

1. First, take both phones to one of your carrier's retail stores and ask if they can help. These stores usually have expensive, non-commercially-available tools that can be used to transfer data. This is really the easiest and cheapest option in most cases.

2. If the store's transfer device isn't compatible with your old phone, and you have a carrier that uses SIM cards (most commonly T-Mobile, AT&T, and Verizon), you can try to save your contacts to your SIM card using your dumb phone and then import them to your Galaxy S5. This will only work if your dumb phone has a contact export feature (so consult its instruction manual), and also uses a Micro SIM card like the Galaxy S5 (many older phones used full-size SIM cards; in that case, this method won't work). If, after consulting your old phone's instruction manual, you are able to export your contacts to your Micro SIM card, pop it back into your Galaxy S5 and go to Contacts → Menu → Settings → Contacts → Import/Export → Import from SIM card. Save the contacts to your Google account.

3. If you happen to have Verizon, you may be able to use its special Backup Assistant feature. Log into your Verizon account online to access it, or call customer service and ask for their help. If you have another carrier, call customer service and ask if they have a solution for your particular case.

4. If none of these methods accomplish what you need, it's time to start Googling. Search Google for **(make and model of your old phone)**

transferring contacts to android. With any luck, you'll find a solution for to your particular situation. Some of them may require spending money on software or computer cables.

5. Failing that, sit down, get comfortable, and manually enter phone numbers into your Contacts app the old-fashioned way. Sorry!

If your old dumb phone has other data besides contacts that you want to transfer, like photos or MP3 files, your best bet will be to consult the phone's instruction manual to learn how to copy those files to an SD memory card. From there, you can copy those files to your computer, and then onto your Galaxy S5's internal memory or external SD card using the techniques in Chapter 7 (p. 251). If your old phone also uses a Micro SD card, you can also try simply putting your old memory card into your Galaxy S5. In many cases, this will work and your Galaxy S5 will automatically detect the relevant content on the memory card.

From Another Android Phone, an Apple iPhone, a Symbian, or a BlackBerry

If you're switching from another smartphone, you are in luck because you can take advantage of Samsung's exclusive Smart Switch program. Samsung realized that its customers wanted an easy and fast way to transfer data to their new phones and created a good, reliable program to do just that.

It runs on both Windows and Mac OS, and allows you to transfer your data from almost any iPhone, Android, BlackBerry, or Symbian phone. In fact, if you are switching from another Android smartphone or from an iPhone and you have an iCloud account, you don't even need to install any desktop software—only the SmartSwitch Android app, available from the Google Play Store.

Whatever your situation is, the Smart Switch website has clear, step-by-step instructions. Start here:

http://www.samsung.com/us/smart-switch/

Chapter 5: Basic Functions

So far, you have learned the basics of the TouchWiz interface: the home screen, the notification panel, the lock screen, and the app drawer. Now, I'll show you how to perform some basic functions such as making phone calls, sending text messages, browsing the Internet, taking pictures and video, and more.

Landscape Mode

Landscape Mode works in pretty much every app—just not on the home screen, app drawer, notification panel, or lock screen. (I don't have an explanation for Samsung's decision on this one.) When you're in an app, just flip your Galaxy S5 sideways and it will automatically enter landscape mode.

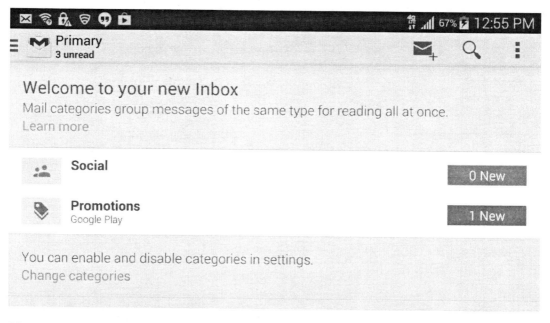

If your Galaxy S5 does not enter landscape mode when you flip it sideways, swipe down the notification panel (p. 54) and make sure the Screen Rotation toggle button is enabled (highlighted in green). You can also use this toggle button to disable landscape mode if you don't want your Galaxy S5 to automatically rotate its screen.

Entering Text

Inputting text is one of the most basic functions you need to know. There are two main ways to do so: using the on-screen keyboard, or using your voice.

Typing With the Keyboard

The default input method for the Galaxy S5 is the Samsung keyboard. In the Android world, there are numerous keyboard options, unlike on the iPhone which limits you to Apple's default keyboard. For example, you can download the official Google Android keyboard from the Google Play Store, or third-party alternatives such as Swype.

In my opinion, however, the Samsung keyboard included with the Galaxy S5 is among the very best. It is fast, accurate, and crucially, includes a row of number keys accessible without first hitting a modifier key. This may sound like an insignificant feature, but it is incredibly convenient in day-to-day use. The Samsung keyboard looks like this:

It is also possible to connect external USB or Bluetooth keyboards to the Galaxy S5, which I discuss in Chapter 10 (p. 297).

There are several important things to know about the Samsung keyboard:

- Tap the shift key to cycle through lowercase, initial uppercase, and caps lock.

- Tap and hold on any character key to bring up the secondary characters displayed in tiny type on each key. Many keys have multiple secondary characters available.

- Tap the "Sym"/"ABC" key to switch between the standard keyboard and symbols.

- As you type, the Galaxy S5 will predict words in the black bar above the keyboard. Tap any word to autocomplete the word you are typing. This can save a lot of typing.

- Tap the microphone key to the immediate right of the "Sym" key once to activate voice input (discussed below), or tap and hold it to access keyboard settings:

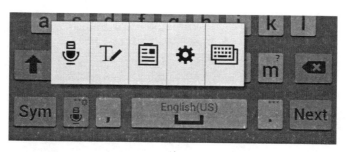

From left to right, these options include:

- Activate Voice Input (same as tapping the microphone key once)

- Activate Handwriting Recognition Mode to write with your fingertips or a capacitive stylus. This feature was copied from the Galaxy Note series, but it feels like an afterthought because the Galaxy S5 does not support the Samsung S Pen. Using a regular stick-type stylus or your fingertips is much less precise than the S Pen and I do not recommend Handwriting Recognition Mode for serious input.

- Show Recent Clipboard Items

- Samsung Keyboard Settings (same as going to Settings → Language and input → Gear icon next to Samsung keyboard)

- Keyboard Type (Normal or floating)

You can input text using the Samsung keyboard by tapping/pecking as you would on a normal keyboard. However, there is another way to type: by swiping.

Swiping for Speedy Input

First released in 2010, the third-party software called Swype was one of the first, if not the first keyboard to offer typing by swiping. Once I tried it, I never looked back. Today, you can still download Swype from the Google Play Store, but you don't need to, because Samsung has included swipe support in its built-in keyboard. I suggest you train yourself to type by swiping, as it is much faster and easier than tapping/pecking.

So how does typing by swiping work? Place your finger on the first character of the word you want, and simply move from letter to letter without letting your finger up. The Galaxy S5 will trace the path of your finger in blue. Here, I am in the process of typing "Hello":

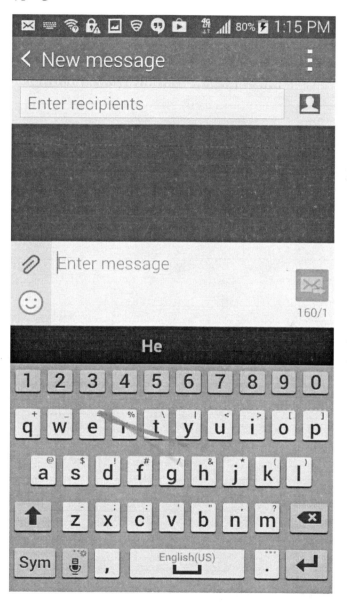

It may take some time to get used to, but in my opinion, it is well worth the effort.

On the Galaxy S5, you can even type multiple words by swiping, without lifting your finger. Simply move your finger over the spacebar in between words.

You can access and change settings for the Samsung keyboard by tapping and holding the microphone key and then tapping the gear icon, or by going to system settings → Language and Input → Gear icon next to "Samsung keyboard." There are many options available to customize features such as auto-prediction and auto-punctuation.

Dictating Text Using Voice Recognition

The other way to input text into your Galaxy S5 is to dictate to it. To activate voice input mode, bring up the Samsung keyboard and single tap the microphone key. You can begin speaking as soon as the following screen appears:

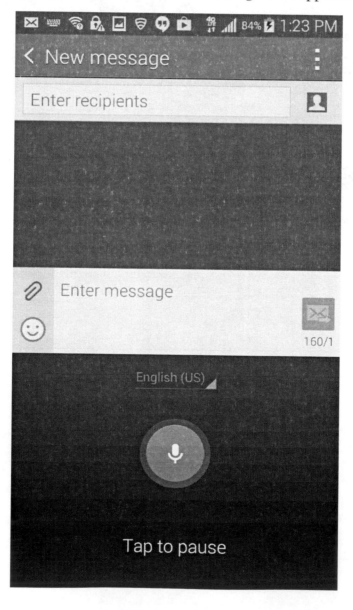

You can tap the microphone icon to pause dictation or tap the dropdown menu above it to change languages. To end dictation, tap the back button. Unlike the Galaxy S5's handwriting recognition mode, which I don't recommend, voice recognition is surprisingly good and Google is improving it all the time. It can be very handy while driving. I suggest you give voice recognition input a shot.

Copy and Paste

The Galaxy S5 makes it easy to copy and paste text. First, you need to select text. Tap and hold on text in apps such as Messages, Gmail, any Internet browser, and so on:

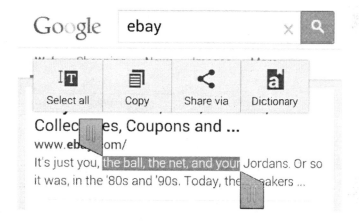

Move the blue tabs around to select the text you want to copy, and then tap "Copy." You can also swipe left and right in this toolbar to access other options. In some apps, you may see the following copy button instead:

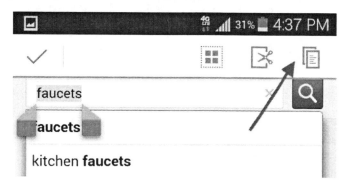

After you have copied your text, tap and hold in the text field you want to paste into, and then tap "Paste." Alternatively, to access data that you previously copied, tap "Clipboard" and then the data you want to paste.

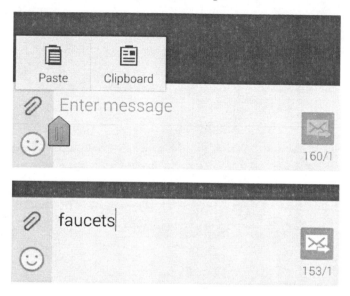

In some apps, you may see the following paste button instead:

Connecting to a Wi-Fi Network

Need to connect to a wireless network at home, in an airport, in a coffee shop, etc.? Make sure the Wi-Fi toggle button is enabled in the notification panel and go to system settings → Wi-Fi. You will see a list of available networks:

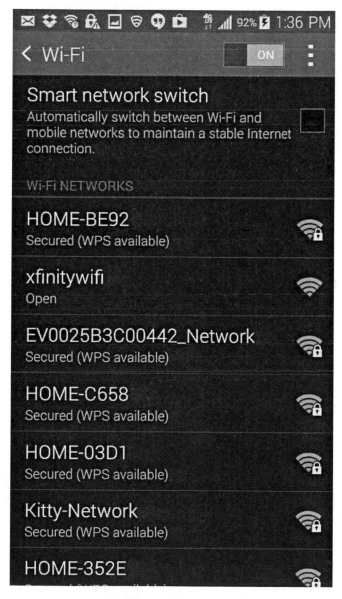

Tap on any network and follow the prompts to connect. If the network is secured, you will be asked to enter a password first.

Alternatively, to connect to a router using WPS technology, tap the WPS button on your router. Then, on your Galaxy S5 tap the menu button in the upper-right-hand corner of the screen and select "WPS push button."

You may see an entry in the list of available networks that says "Add Wi-Fi network." This option is only necessary if you are adding a network that is out of range or does not broadcast an SSID. You'll probably never need to use this option. If your network does not appear in the list, try toggling Wi-Fi off and on again.

> For some commercial Wi-Fi hotspots, such as the ones at Starbucks, you will be able to connect to the network without a password, but after you're connected you'll need to open your browser and accept terms & conditions before you actually get Internet access. You will usually receive a notification in your notification panel that you need to log in, but not always. So, if you connect to a public Wi-Fi hotspot but data isn't working, open your browser and try to load a web page. You should be redirected to a login page, and after logging in, you will have Internet access.

Browsing the Internet

By default, the Galaxy S5 comes with two Internet browsers. The first is aptly titled "Internet," and the second is the mobile version of Google Chrome. Although the stock Internet browser is not a bad app, you'll want to skip it and go straight to Chrome. Chrome is updated more often, is faster, and integrates with your Google account to sync your bookmarks and browser tabs with your desktop computer running Chrome. Even if you don't use Chrome on your desktop computer (which you should), in my opinion it's still preferable to the stock Internet browser.

You'll find Chrome in your app drawer. If, for some reason, your Galaxy S5 did not come with Chrome, simply download it free from the Google Play Store.

Upon opening Chrome for the first time, you'll need to accept Google's Terms of Service to continue. Do so, and then on the next screen sign in with your Google account. You'll see a help screen like the following—take the tour to learn about Chrome's major features.

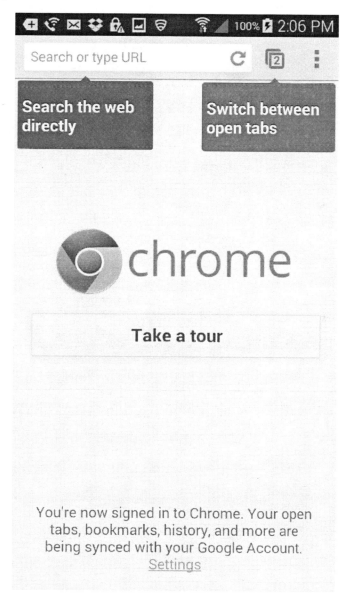

To browse the web, you can enter web addresses (.com's, etc.) in the search box at the top of the screen, or simply enter words to search Google. While browsing, you can double-tap paragraphs to auto-zoom, pinch with two fingers to zoom manually, copy and paste (p. 77) text, and tap and hold links to bring up additional options. Refresh pages using the circular arrow inside the search box.

Tabbed Browsing

You can have multiple tabs open at the same time, much like on a desktop browser. This is a convenient way to jump back and forth between web pages or save pages for later viewing. To see your open tabs, tap the number in the upper-right-hand corner of the screen.

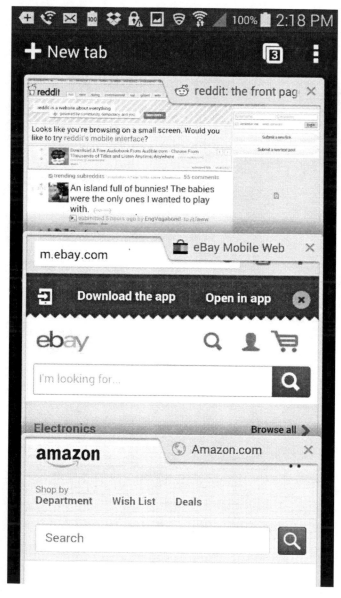

Tap a tab to open it, or create a new tab with the "New tab" button.

Adding and Viewing Bookmarks

To bookmark an open web page, tap the menu button and then the star icon. Hit "Save." To manage your bookmarks, tap the menu button and then "Bookmarks."

Tap on folders to open them, and tap the back button to go to the previous folder. Tap and hold individual bookmarks to rename them ("Edit bookmark") or to delete them. There is no way to move bookmarks between folders on the Galaxy S5. You will either need to use the Bookmark Manager on the desktop version of Chrome, or delete the bookmarks and recreate them in the correct folder one at a time.

Private Browsing With Incognito Mode

Sometimes, you might want to visit web pages without leaving a trace in your history, especially since Chrome synchronizes your history and open pages with your desktop computer. No judgment. To do so, tap the menu key and select "New Incognito Tab." This new tab, which will have a blue background, will let you browse without permanently storing your history, cookies, or any other sign of the web pages you visit.

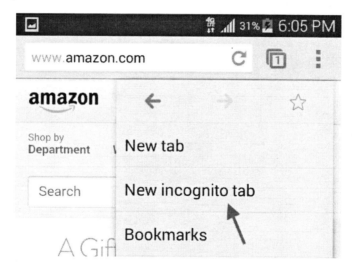

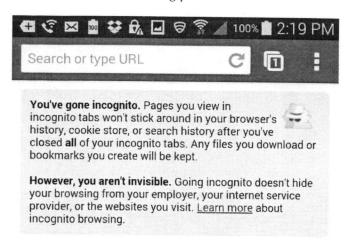

Viewing Open Tabs on Your Desktop Computer

As long as your desktop version of Google Chrome is set to sync open tabs (in Chrome's "Advanced Sync Settings"), you can access them from anywhere using your Galaxy S5. To do so, tap the menu key and select "Other devices." You'll see a list of devices synced with your Google account—look for your desktop computer and tap the tab you want to open it on your Galaxy S5.

Overriding Mobile Web Themes

While some websites have great mobile versions, others are just detestable, broken messes. Not all websites and business are up to date with the importance of functioning mobile websites. If this happens, you can attempt to override the website's mobile theme by tapping the menu key and selecting "Request Desktop Site." This doesn't work in all cases, but it usually does.

Extensions: Nope

One very popular feature of the desktop Chrome browser is its vast library of extensions, such as ad blockers and password managers. Although there is often speculation about if and when Google will roll out extension support for the Android version of Chrome, at this time there is no way to run Chrome extensions on your Galaxy S5.

Clearing History and Cookies

To clear your private browsing data, go to Chrome's three-dot menu → Settings → Privacy. Tap "Clear browsing data" at the bottom of the screen, select the types of data you want to delete, and then tap "Clear."

Calls

Calls on the Galaxy S5 are made through the Phone app. It is in your app tray and app drawer by default.

Making and Ending Calls

To place a call, tap the Phone app shortcut and then the "Keypad" tab.

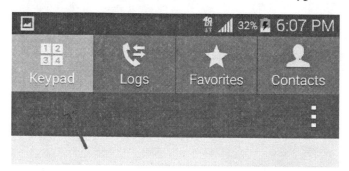

Dial the outgoing number as you would on a normal phone, and then tap the green dial button below the zero key. If you make an error while entering the number, tap the light blue backspace arrow below the pound ("#") key.

There are several other ways to make calls as well:

- Tap the "Logs" tab to view recent calls, tap the contact's name, and then the green dial button.

- Tap the "Favorites" tab to view your most frequently called contacts, tap the contact's name, and then the green dial button.

- Tap the "Contacts" tab to view your entire phone book, tap the contact's name, and then the green dial button.

- To speed dial a contact, see the section below entitled, "Speed Dial."

- Voice dial contacts using Google Now (p. 166) or S Voice (p. 180).

- Tap a 10-digit phone number in an Internet browser, and then the green dial button.

> Swipe left on any contact in your call log or Contacts to quickly text message them, or swipe right to call them.

Answering and Rejecting Calls

To answer an incoming call, tap and hold on the green phone icon, and drag it right. To reject an incoming call, tap and hold on the red phone icon, and drag it left.

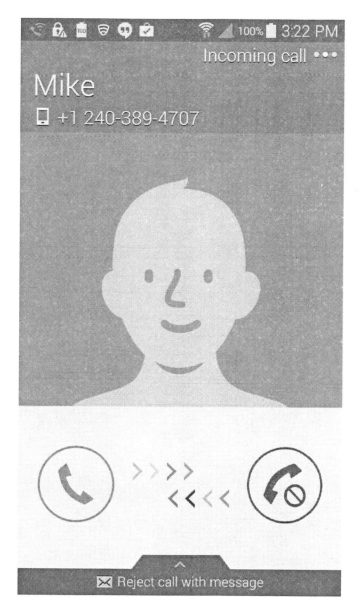

Alternatively, swipe the "Reject call with message" tab upward, and then tap a gray button next to the message you wish to send. Your Galaxy S5 will decline the call and dispatch a text message to the caller.

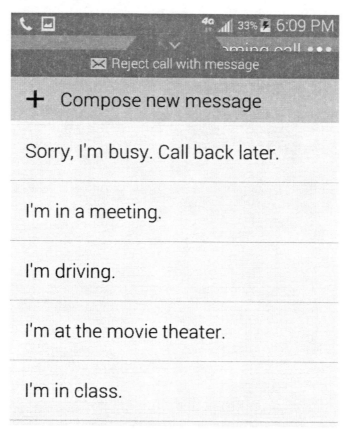

To add a custom message, tap the "Compose new message" button or go to system settings → Call → Call Rejection → Set up call rejection messages.

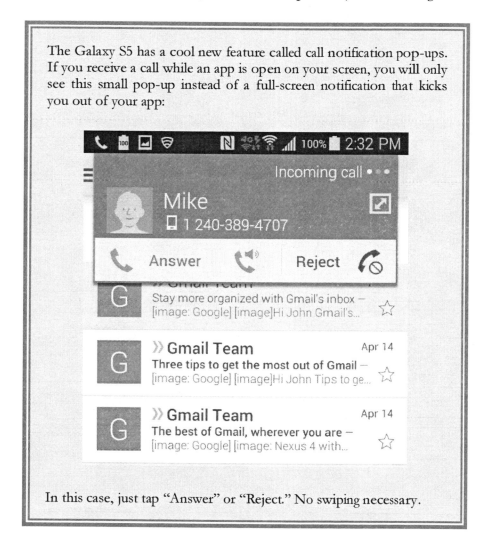

In-Call Controls

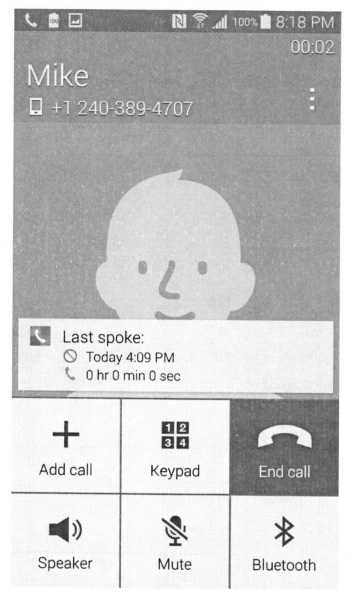

Once you're in an active call, you have the options shown above. "Keypad" brings up a number pad so you can enter numbers on automated phone lines. "Speaker" switches to speakerphone. "Mute" turns off your microphone, so the other party cannot hear you." "Bluetooth" switches the call to a Bluetooth headset or car stereo, if <u>one has been configured</u> (p. 198).

You can also adjust the call volume using the Volume Up and Down buttons, or tap the home button to see your home screen and open other apps while staying on the line. Additionally, you can tap the three-dot menu icon to see additional call options, such as Hold, Extra Volume, and more.

Screening Calls Discreetly

Sometimes, you might want to discretely reject a call—let it go to voicemail, but let it ring normally first. Obviously all you have to do is not answer—but there's a good trick to know. When the Galaxy S5 is ringing, just tap the Volume Down key to silence the ringtone, but let the call continue to voicemail normally. This way, the caller won't think you're rejecting their call after one or two rings, and you won't have to listen to the phone ring all the way to voicemail.

Handling Missed Calls

If you miss a call, you will receive a notification in your notification panel. Swipe down the notification panel and tap the notification to view the caller's details and return their call if you wish.

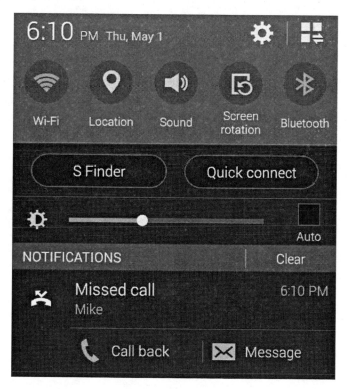

Speed Dial

To create a new speed dial contact, go to the Phone app and tap the "Keypad" tab. Tap the menu button and then "Speed dial." From this page, tap the numeral to which you wish to assign a contact and select the appropriate contact/phone number.

To dial a speed dial contact, go to the Phone app and tap the "Keypad" tab. Dial the speed dial number, holding the last digit until the contact is dialed. For example, to dial the contact associated with speed dial "2," simply tap and hold 2. To dial the contact associated with speed dial "25," tap 2, then tap and hold 5.

To replace or remove a speed dial contact, go to the Phone app and tap the "Keypad" tab. Tap the menu button and then "Speed dial." From this page, tap and hold the contact you wish to remove or reassign, and then select the desired option and follow the prompts.

Checking Voicemail

To check your voicemail, go to the Phone app and tap the "Keypad" tab. Tap the cassette tape icon below the star ("*") key and follow the prompts. The first time you call your voicemail, you may need to set a PIN and greeting depending on your carrier's procedures.

Visual Voicemail

Depending on your carrier, you may have a visual voicemail app in your app drawer. This will display your voicemails in list form on the screen, rather than requiring you to listen to your voicemails and press number commands. If your carrier supports this option, try it out—it's a big step up.

Sending Text Messages (SMS) and Picture Messages (MMS)

Text messages on the Galaxy S5 are sent through the Messages app. It is in your app tray and app drawer by default.

After you have opened the Messages app, tap the pen and paper icon in the upper-right-hand corner of the screen to compose a new text message.

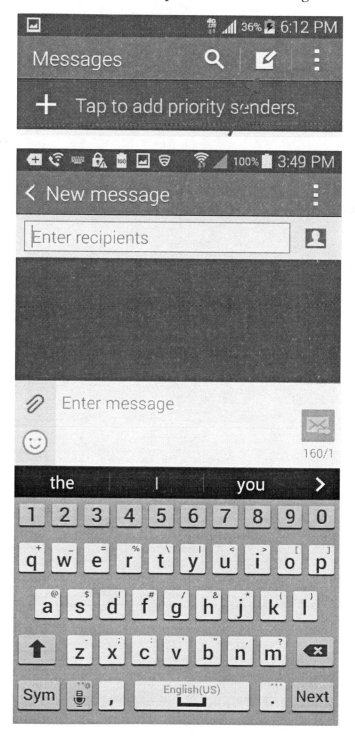

To select a recipient, tap in the "Enter recipients" field and type a phone number or name in your contacts. Alternatively, tap the button to the right of the "Enter recipient" field and select a contact from your phone book. You can enter multiple recipients. Some carriers support group messaging, so if you include multiple recipients, any replies sent to you will also be sent to all of your original recipients. Be careful with this feature—it can be very useful, but potentially very awkward if you don't know it exists.

To enter a message, tap in the "Enter message" field and type your message. You can attach a media file (image, voice recording, etc.) by tapping the paper clip icon to the left of the "enter message" field, selecting "Image," opening the Gallery "Just Once," selecting a picture, and tapping "Done." This is how to send a picture message, otherwise known as an MMS.

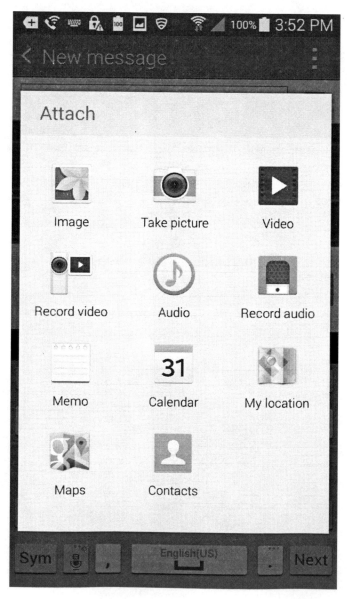

Once you have selected a recipient and composed your message, tap the orange envelope icon to the right of the message composition box to send your message. You do not have to enter a message to send a picture.

When you receive a response to a text message, you will receive a notification in your notification panel, as well as a helpful bubble icon in the Messages app.

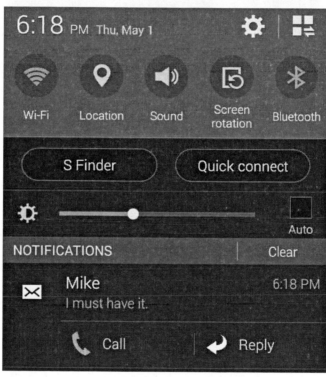

Tap the entry in your Messages app, or in your notification panel to open the text message thread.

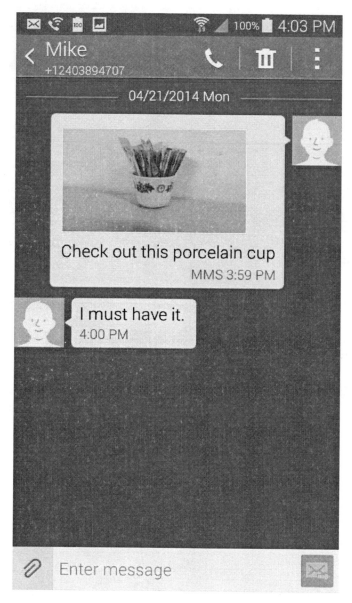

Compose further replies in the same manner as described above.

Setting Up Priority Senders to Text Quickly

Priority Senders is a new feature in the Galaxy S5 Messages app that lets you compose new texts to your favorite people with a single tap. To set it up, tap "+ Tap to add priority senders" in the Messages app.

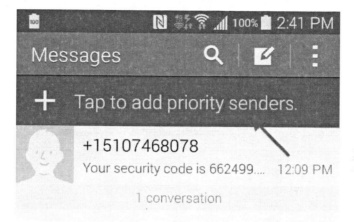

Next, tap "Contacts." Check any contacts that you wish to place in your Priority Senders area. Finally, tap "Done" in the upper-right-hand corner of the screen. Your contact(s) will appear in the Priority Senders area. Tap one to quickly compose a new text message, or tap the plus sign to add additional Priority Senders.

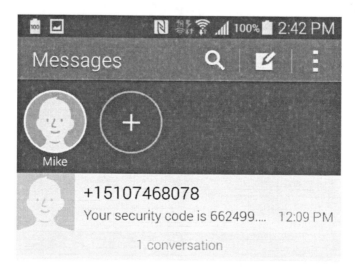

Using the Gmail App

On the Galaxy S5, there are two apps from which you can send and receive e-mails. The first is the Gmail app, which is optimized for Gmail users. For a majority of Android users, this will probably be your only, or at least most commonly used, email app. The second option is the Email app, which is compatible with any POP3 or IMAP mailbox. You may find the Email app useful if you have a non-Gmail e-mail account that you use frequently.

Setting Up the Gmail Inbox

Before you can use the Gmail app, you will need to set up a Google account on your Galaxy S5. Most of you probably did this during initial setup, as described in Chapter 3 (p. 17). If you did not, launching the Gmail app will prompt you to do so. Unlike the Phone and Messages apps, the Gmail app is not in your app tray by default. You can access it in your app drawer. I suggest creating a shortcut (p. 67) on your home screen or in your app tray if you plan to use Gmail extensively. When you first launch Gmail, you will see a screen like this:

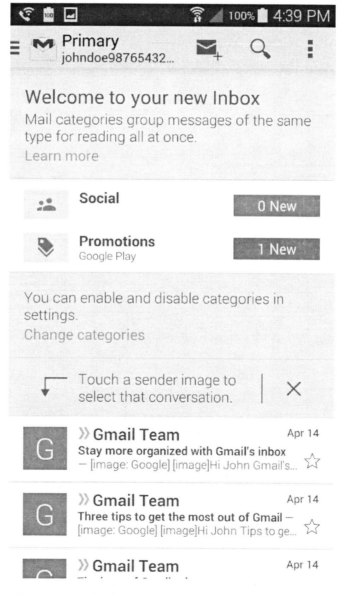

If you use Gmail on your desktop computer, you are probably already familiar with Gmail's categories. By default, Gmail gives you a "Primary" inbox, plus a "Social" and "Promotions" inbox. It automatically places any emails from social networks (e.g., Facebook) into "Social," and advertisements into "Promotions." You can enable or disable these categories, and others, by tapping "Change categories." Personally, I disable all of these categories so all of my mail goes into my Primary inbox, but you may do whatever suits you. When you're done, swipe the "Welcome to your new Inbox" panel left or right to clear it, and tap the "X" on the "Touch a sender…" message. Your Gmail inbox will be ready to use.

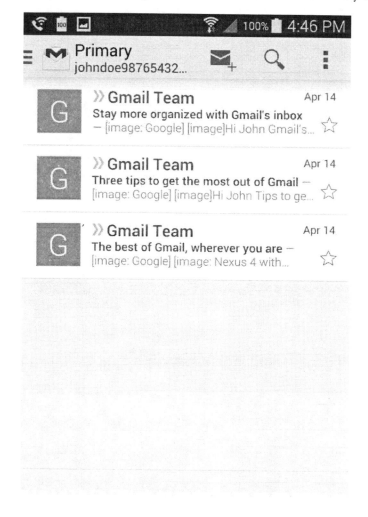

Let's discuss the controls available in the inbox.

- Tap on any email to open, view, and reply to it.

- Swipe an email left or right to archive it.

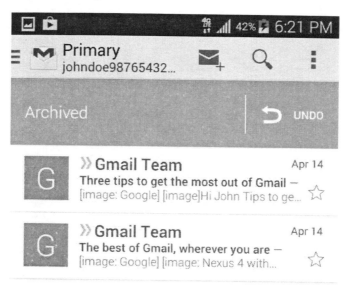

- Tap the colored letters on the left-hand side of the screen to select emails. Then, use the controls along the top of the screen to choose what to do with the selected emails. From left to right, these buttons include: exit selection mode (checkmark), archive, trash, mark as read/unread, and menu. The three-dot menu button includes many other options such as starring, marking as important, and so on.

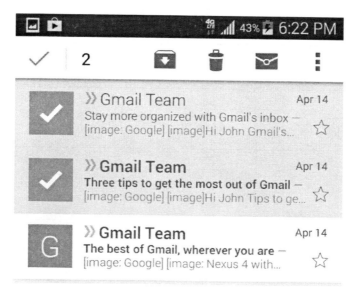

- Swipe from the far left edge of the screen right, or tap the red envelope in the upper-left-hand corner of the screen to pull up the toolbar. From here, you can swipe up and down to scroll, and tap to select the account, folder, or label you want to open.

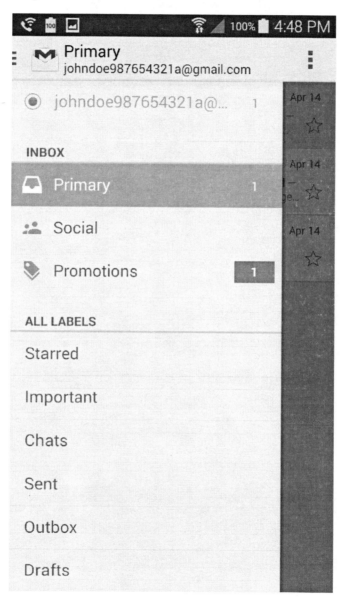

- Tap the gray envelope with a plus (+) sign in the upper-right-hand corner of the screen to compose a new email. Send the email with the gray triangle button.

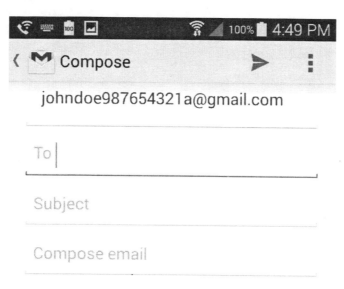

- Finally, you can tap the magnifying glass icon in the upper-right-hand corner of the screen to search your Gmail account.

Reading an Email

When reading an email, the controls at the top of the screen include, from left to right:

- Red Envelope: Back to inbox.

- Folder: Archive email.

- Trashcan: Delete email.

- Gray Envelope: Mark as unread.

- Three dots: Menu with additional options.

Reply with the left-pointing arrow, or reply-all or forward the email with the three-dot menu. You can also tap the tiny down carat to display sender and recipient information. Tap the purple (or other colored) letter to view and/or create a contact associated with the email's sender.

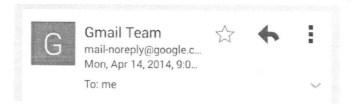

You can also pinch with two fingers to zoom in and out on the email body itself.

Composing and Sending an Email

Upon choosing to create a new message, reply, reply-all, or forward an email, you will be presented with a composition screen like this:

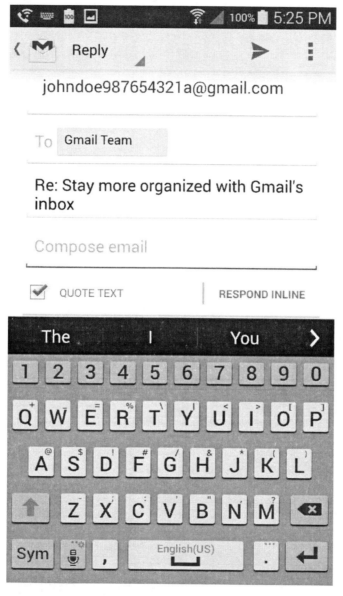

Tap "Reply" to change the mode of your email (reply, reply-all, or forward). Below, you can add or remove recipients in the "To" field, and edit the subject if you wish. Compose your email in the "Compose email" field. The right-facing gray arrow to the left of the three-dot menu will send the email.

Attaching Files

On older Android phones, it was only possible to attach image or video files to Gmail messages. Fortunately, this has since been corrected, and it is possible to attach nearly any type of file saved on your Galaxy S5, in your Dropbox, or in your Google Drive. To attach a file to a Gmail message, tap the three-dot menu button on the composition screen and then "Attach file." Use the following screen to find and select the file you wish to attach.

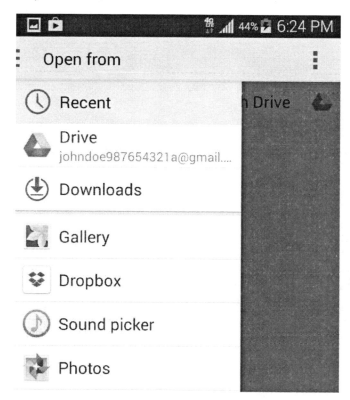

If the file you want to attach is saved in an odd directory and you can't find it from this prompt, there is <u>another way to attach files to Gmail messages</u> (p. 193).

Refreshing Your Inbox

Sometimes, the Gmail app gets clogged up and stops receiving new emails. If this happens, bring it back into sync by tapping the menu button in the Inbox and selecting "Refresh." Sometimes this does not fix the problem, however, and in that case you'll need to restart your Galaxy S5. Also, sometimes emails with large attachments get stuck in the Outbox and the only way to get them to send is to restart the phone. These problems don't happen all the time, but often enough you should be aware of them.

Storing More Emails Offline

By default, the Galaxy S5 stores your last 30 days of messages on its internal memory. For anything older than that, it has to connect to Google's servers. If you spend a lot of time in areas without an Internet connection, consider increasing this setting in the Gmail menu → Settings → (Your email address) → Days of Mail to Sync.

Getting a Notification for Every New Email

By default, if you receive multiple emails in a short period of time, your Galaxy S5 will sound a notification only the first time. This can be bad if there is an urgent chain of emails, because you might not realize you've received more than one message. To make your Galaxy S5 sound a notification for every single new email, go to the Gmail menu → (Your email address) → Inbox Sound & Vibrate and check "Notify for Every Message."

Disabling Swipe-to-Archive to Prevent Accidents

As I showed you earlier, by default you can swipe an email in your inbox right or left to archive it. While this is convenient, unfortunately it is far too easy to accidentally swipe a message away and miss the short window to tap "Undo." Unlike accidentally deleting an email, there is no way to know which email you archived this way! There have been many times where I accidentally archived an email that I knew was important, but couldn't figure out what it was. To prevent this, go to the Gmail menu → Settings → General Settings and disable "Swipe to Archive."

Auto-Fitting Messages

To make messages conform to the screen size of your Galaxy S5, go to the Gmail menu → Settings → General Settings and enable "Auto-Fit Messages." Without this setting enabled, you will often have to pan left and right to read emails that are wider than your screen.

Confirming Before Sending

In a professional setting, few things are worse than sending an email you didn't mean to send. To avoid this, go to the Gmail menu → Settings → General Settings and enable "Confirm Before Sending." You'll receive a confirmation dialog every time you attempt to send a message, preventing a potential classic career-ending faux pas. Just make sure not to accidentally reply-all—the other classic email mistake.

Customizing Your Inbox Categories

Google recently introduced a Gmail feature that splits your inbox into various tabs such as "Social" and "Promotional." If you detest this feature as much as I do, it's easy to switch off. Go to the Gmail menu → Settings → (Your email address) → Inbox Categories and uncheck the categories you don't want.

Setting a Signature

To set a signature for all emails sent from your Galaxy S5, go to the Gmail menu → Settings → (Your email address) → Signature.

Muting Conversations

The Gmail app includes a "muting" feature, which will automatically archive all future emails in a given conversation, skipping your inbox entirely. This is a great feature if you've been CC'd on an ongoing email thread you don't care about. To mute a conversation, open it, tap the menu key, and then "Mute."

Using the Email App for Non-Gmail Accounts

As I mentioned earlier, the Email app is only necessary if you frequently use a non-Gmail account. It supports all POP3 and IMAP mailboxes. If this means nothing to you, feel free to skip this section. But if you do want to set up a non-Gmail account, Email is the app you want. You will be prompted to create an account upon opening Email for the first time:

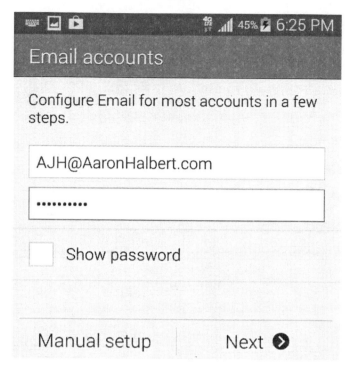

Enter your account information and proceed through the setup process. The email app has pre-loaded settings for common email providers such as Yahoo, but if you are adding a work or school email account, consult your system administrator/IT department to get the proper configuration information. If you are adding an email account from a webmail service that is not pre-loaded into the Galaxy S5, consult its FAQ or Help section to get the proper configuration information.

Once you have properly configured your account, you will be taken to the Email app's main menu. Tap "Inbox" to start reading your email.

> If you use Microsoft Outlook at work, I strongly recommend you purchase and use the app TouchDown. It is a fantastic, full-featured Outlook client for Android, and keeps all of your work information nicely contained in one app. Read more about it here (p. 294).

Taking Photos

Photos and video are taken using the Camera app, which you will find in your app drawer. The Galaxy S5 has a 16-megapixel rear camera with a 31mm equivalent f/2.2 lens and 1/2.6" sensor, as well as a 2-megapixel front camera.

> The Galaxy S5 features a new way to quickly access your Camera from the lock screen. When you power the device on, you will see a camera icon in the lower-right-hand corner of the lock screen. Drag it upwards and release to quickly open the Camera app without having to unlock your phone first. (Fortunately, this is not a security risk; you can't view any pictures already stored on the phone this way, or do anything except take new pictures.)

By default, the Camera app opens into camera (as opposed to video) mode. Let's discuss the features available on this screen.

1. Open camera settings (selected features discussed below).

2. Enable/disable HDR mode. HDR stands for "High Dynamic Range," and uses software techniques to improve the exposure and color in your photos. Basically, digital cameras can capture only a portion of the lighting situations that the human eye can see, and HDR tries to correct this. If your photo includes both very bright and very dark objects, you will normally get either some over-exposed, blown out areas, or some under-exposed, dark areas, or both. HDR can help fix this problem. Experiment with this setting to see what looks best.

3. Enable/disable selective focus mode. Everyone likes bokeh, the blurred-background effect commonly seen in portrait photography. Selective focus mode not only helps you get better bokeh in your photos, it also allows you to change the focus point of your image after it's been taken. More discussion of selective focus mode can be found <u>below</u> (p. 117).

4. Switch between the rear and front cameras.

5. The autofocus and metering area. The camera will focus on whatever you place in this circle.

6. Open the Gallery app to view previously taken photos.

7. Choose from a variety of camera modes, including beauty face, panorama, dual camera, and more. You can also tap "Download" to download more mode plug-ins from Samsung.

8. Shutter button. Takes a picture.

9. Video button. Switches out of camera mode and into video mode, and starts recording.

Finally, you can pinch with two fingers to zoom in or out. Zooming is accomplished digitally, not optically, so the quality will degrade fairly quickly as you zoom in.

Using Burst Shot to Capture Fast Action

The Galaxy S5 is capable of taking multiple shots in rapid succession, which is useful for fast action scenes. To enable burst shot, open the extended Camera settings as described above and change "Burst Shots" to "On." *where? Mode?*

Tagging Your Photos With Location Data

Ever take a photo and forget where you took it? You can eliminate this problem using the Galaxy S5's location tagging. It embeds GPS coordinates in the metadata of your photos. To enable it, open the Camera settings, swipe down, and tap "Location tags" to turn it on. You can view these coordinates using an advanced image viewer like Lightroom on a PC, or by viewing the photo in the Gallery app, tapping the three-dot menu button, and selecting "More info."

If you enable this feature, remember that GPS information will be embedded in any photos you post online! This feature can be useful, but be careful not to cause yourself any privacy problems by, say, distributing photos with your home's GPS coordinates embedded in them. Also, keep in mind that this feature will only fully work as long as your Location toggle button is switched on in your <u>notification</u>

panel (p. 54), and you granted apps permission to access your location when first setting up your Galaxy S5.

Using the Entire Screen as a Shutter Button

Sometimes, tapping the tiny on-screen shutter button to take a shot is clumsy. Fortunately, it's possible to configure the entire image preview area to function as a huge shutter button. To do so, open the Camera settings and enable "Tap to take pics."

Self-Timer

The self-timer mode is very useful for taking group shots. To use it, open the Camera settings, swipe down, and enable "Timer." Choose your preferred duration. Now, the tricky part is taking the picture without a tripod…

Flipping Front Camera Images Automatically

By default, the Galaxy S5 takes pictures using the front camera in mirror-image mode, meaning that you will see the same image you see in a regular mirror. Of course, this is not how other people see you! To see yourself in others' eyes, enter front camera mode, open the Camera settings, and change "Save As Flipped" to "On."

Freeing Internal Memory by Storing Photos on Your SD Card

The first time you open the Camera app with an SD card inserted you'll be prompted to switch storage to it (except for burst shots, which must be stored on internal memory because of the speed requirement). Enable this feature to prevent your Galaxy S5's internal memory from getting filled with image files. If you didn't change this setting when you first launched your Camera app, just open Camera settings, swipe down, and change "Storage" to "Memory card."

Muting the Shutter Sound

Sometimes you need to take pictures discreetly. Creepy, but OK. To disable the shutter sound, open the Camera settings, swipe down, and change "Shutter sound" to "Off."

Taking Panoramic Shots

To take a panoramic shot (super-wide-angle), for example of a landscape, tap the Mode button to the left of the shutter button and tap the Panorama option. Aim your Galaxy S5 at the far left or right edge of the scene you want to capture. Tap the shutter button once, and then slowly move your Galaxy S5 across the scene. Tap the stop button when you're finished, and then tap the thumbnail in the lower-left-hand corner of the screen to see your new panoramic shot. Voila! Note that you'll need to tap the Mode button again to put your Galaxy S5 back into the default Auto mode.

Taking HDR Shots

As I noted earlier, the Galaxy S5 has a faux-HDR mode that simulates the high-saturation, high-dynamic range shots that have recently become popular among digital photographers. To use it, tap the sun and moon icon at the top of the screen so that it says "On." This icon is #2 in the screenshot I provided earlier.

Getting Great Bokeh and Edit Bokeh Using Selective Focus

Selective focus mode helps you do two different but related things. First, it helps you take a photo of an object or person with a blurred background. Second, it allows you to change the point of focus after the photo has already been taken, i.e., to blur the foreground and bring the background into focus. To enable Selective focus mode, tap the icon at the top of the screen with two silhouettes, so that it says "On."

For selective focus mode to work best, the object in the foreground must be within 1.5 feet of the Galaxy S5's camera, and the background must be at least 4.5 feet beyond the object.

Once you have enabled Selective focus mode, take a picture and hold the Galaxy S5 still while it instructs you to do so. Afterwards, when you view the photo full-screen in your Gallery app, you will see the Selective focus icon. Tap it to select foreground focus, background focus, or pan-focus (everything in focus).

Instagram-Like Effects, Including Sepia, Vintage, and Grayscale

The Galaxy S5's camera app has several built-in filters that can give your photos Instagram-like effects. To use these, go to the camera settings, tap "Effects," and choose the one you want.

Setting the Flash Mode

By default, the Galaxy S5's flash is off. In camera settings, you can set it to On (always), Off (always), or Auto (triggers only when necessary).

Using Voice Commands to Take Photos

A final cool trick with the Galaxy S5's camera is voice command. When you turn Voice control on in the camera settings, you can take photos by saying "Smile," "Cheese," "Capture," or "Shoot." This can be handy instead of the self-timer to take group shots, or to make your shots even steadier by eliminating the need to tap the screen to take a picture.

Capturing Video

To enter video mode, tap the video camera icon in the lower-right-hand corner of the viewfinder screen.

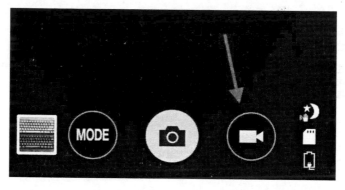

Recording will begin as soon as you enter video mode. Tap the pause icon to pause recording, or the stop icon to stop recording and save the video. Tap the camera icon to return to camera mode. Counter-intuitively, you must be in camera mode to make changes to settings for video mode.

Taking 4K (UHD) Video

One of the selling points of the Galaxy S5 is its ability to capture 4K video for playback on the latest high-resolution TVs. But, there's no clear option to do so in the Camera app. What you need to do is open the camera settings, tap "Video size," and change the resolution to 3840x2160 pixels. That's 4K!

Taking Slow-Mo and Fast-Mo Video

To take slow-motion or fast-motion video, tap the settings button while in Camera mode, tap "Recording mode," and choose the desired setting.

Enabling Video Stabilization

By default, the Galaxy S5's video image stabilization feature is turned off. This feature reduces shake and improves video quality in low-light settings. To enable it, go to camera settings and tap "Video stabilization" to turn it on.

Viewing and Editing Photos & Videos

So, you've taken some photos or videos using the Camera app and now you want to view them. To do so, use the Gallery app. You can either access it from your app drawer, or, from the Camera app itself. From the Camera app, tap the small square in the lower-right-hand corner of the shutter view to open the Gallery.

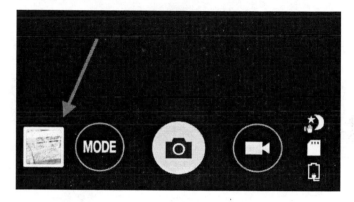

Below is a view of the main Gallery screen. In it, swipe up and down to view your photos and videos, sorted by newest to oldest. Tap any thumbnail to open it in full-screen view (or play a video), and use the back button to return to the main screen. Tap and hold any thumbnail to select it and enter selection mode.

In selection mode, you can select multiple photos by tapping on their thumbnails. Once selected, tap the trashcan icon in the upper-right-hand corner of the screen to delete the photos, or tap the three-dot menu icon to select other actions like mass rotating or copying. You can also tap the Share Via (p. 180) icon to email or otherwise share the selected photos with friends or family.

In the screenshot below, I have tapped and selected three thumbnails, indicated by the three check marks.

Below is a photo in full-screen mode. Tap anywhere on the photo itself to hide the menu bars, or swipe the bottom menu bar left and right to view more thumbnails.

Editing Photos and Videos in the Studio

The Galaxy S5 has a new feature for editing photos and videos called the Studio. It is much more powerful than the editing tools included in earlier Galaxy S devices. For example, it allows you to:

- Rotate, crop, and resize photos

- Adjust contrast and brightness

- Remove red eye

- Add frames

- Draw on your photos

- Trim video clips

- Apply filters to video clips

- … and much more.

To access the Studio, tap the three-dot menu icon in the Gallery and then "Studio."

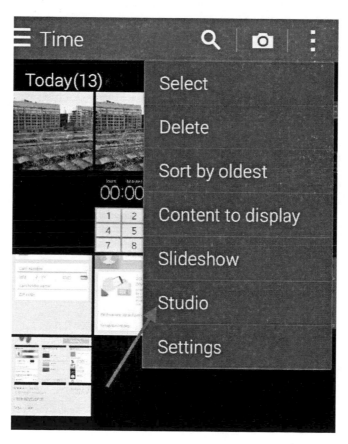

Then, tap the appropriate option on the Studio's home screen.

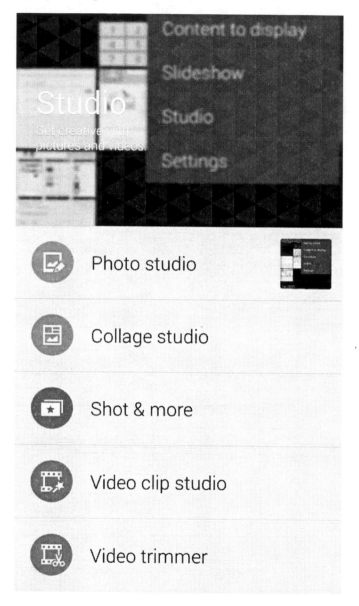

Managing Contacts

The Contacts app is your phone book. Use it to store names, numbers, email addresses, and other contact information for your friends, family, and business contacts.

You can access the Contacts app in a couple of different ways. You'll find it in your app tray by default, and you can also access it by opening the Phone app and then tapping the Contacts tab in the upper-right-hand corner of the screen.

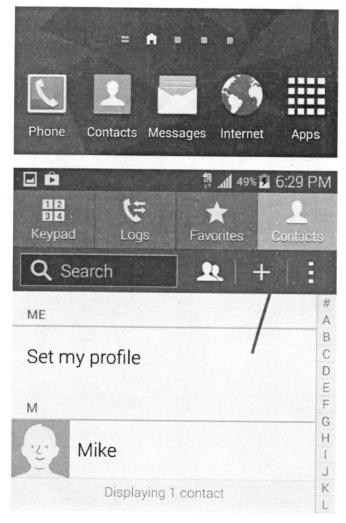

Swipe up and down to scroll through your contacts, or tap a letter along the right edge of the screen to skip to that section. Tap a contact to view his or her details.

Adding New Contacts

To add a new contact, tap the plus (+) icon next to the Search box, as shown in the screenshot above. You will need to select the account in which to save the contact. I strongly suggest you keep all contacts saved to your Google account, so they will be consolidated in one place and will be restored automatically if you ever lose your data or your Galaxy S5. You may see a pop-up box suggesting that you need to save your contacts to a Samsung account for them to be backed up. Don't believe this propaganda from Samsung. Although they would like you to use a Samsung account, it's much better to consolidate your contacts in your Google account, and they will indeed be backed up. As I have previously noted, a Samsung account is an unnecessary add-on feature (p. 28).

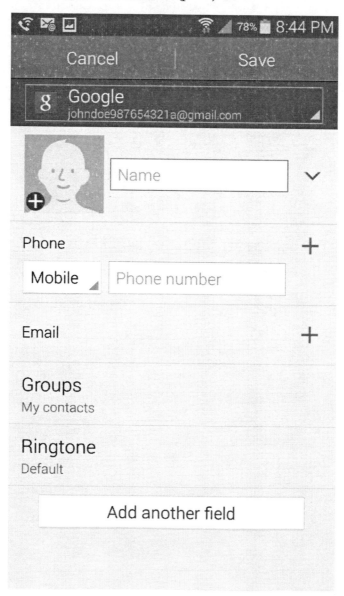

Enter the contact's information. Tap a green plus sign to add additional fields to the record, and tap the face icon to assign a photo from your Gallery to the contact. You can also change where the contact is stored by tapping the large dropdown that says "Google." Again, I strongly recommend you save all contacts to your Google account. Once you have entered all the contact's information, tap "Save."

Editing Existing Contacts

To edit a contact's details, tap the contact's name to open his or her details, and then tap the pencil icon in the upper-right-hand corner of the screen.

Deleting Contacts

To delete a contact, tap and hold the contact's name in the main list view, check any other contacts you wish to delete, and then tap the trashcan icon.

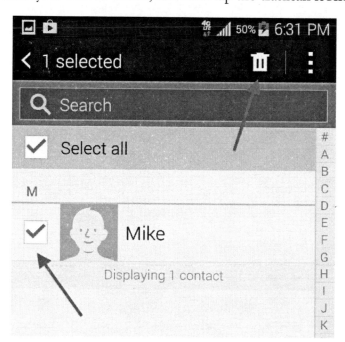

Linking Duplicate Contacts

When duplicates occur in your Google contact database, you can easily merge them by opening your Gmail account on your desktop PC, opening your contacts, and using the Find & Merge Duplicates feature.

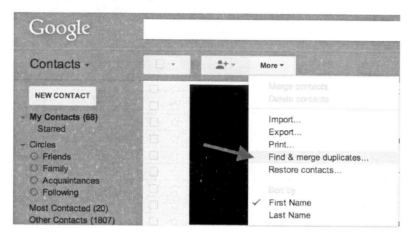

However, sometimes apps on your Galaxy S5 like Facebook or LinkedIn will create duplicate entries. Since these are from different sources and are not saved to Google's servers, Google's contact tools will not help you. Instead, you can use the Galaxy S5's built-in "Link Contact" feature, which allows you to manage multiple contacts as a single contact. (However, it does not actually merge the two records, which is why Google's Find & Merge Duplicates feature is preferable.)

To use this feature, tap the three-dot menu icon in the Contacts app and select "Link contacts." Then, select the contacts you want to link and tap "Done." Note that you can only link contacts with the same name.

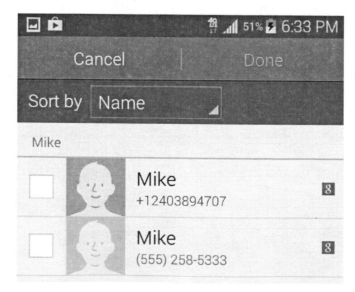

To unlink contacts, open a linked contact and tap the chain-link button. Tap the minus signs next to each contact you want to unlink, and then press the back button to exit this screen.

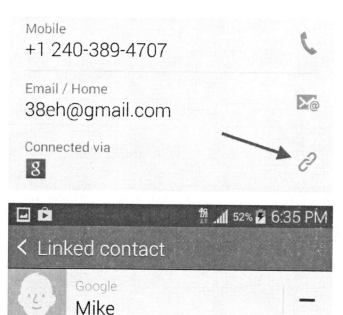

Sharing Contacts

To share a contact in the standard vCard format, tap on a contact in your contact list. Then, tap on the three-dot menu and select "Share name card." Choose any method you wish, such as SMS or e-mail.

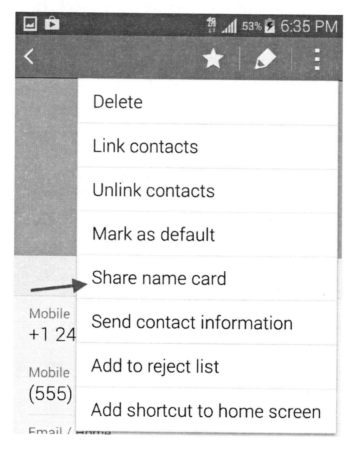

Setting Custom Ringtones for Contacts

To assign a custom ringtone for a contact, first get an MP3, WAV, AAC, Amazon MP3, or similar file of the ringtone or song you want and save it somewhere on your Galaxy S5 or its SD card. If you have an audio file on your desktop or laptop computer, email it to yourself as an attachment and then save it using the Gmail app. It does not matter what folder you save the file to.

Once you have an audio file on your Galaxy S5, download the app, "Ringtone Maker," from the Google Play Store. This app will let you customize the portion of the song that plays when you get a call (e.g., the chorus).

Once you open Ringtone Maker, tap the green arrow next to the song you want to use as a ringtone. Tap "Edit."

After you tap "Edit," you will see the following screen. Move the sliders around to choose the portion of the song to use for your ringtone. (Press the play button to preview the clip.)

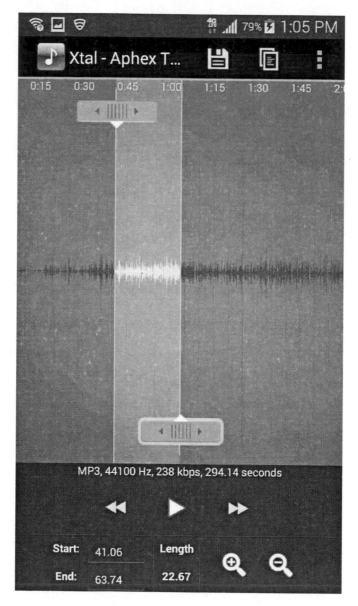

Once you are happy with your selection, tap the disk icon in the upper-right-hand corner of the screen.

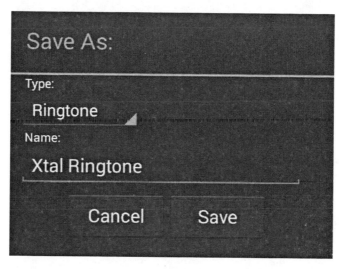

Rename your ringtone if you wish and tap "Save." Finally, choose whether you want to make it your default ringtone for all contacts, or assign it only to a single contact.

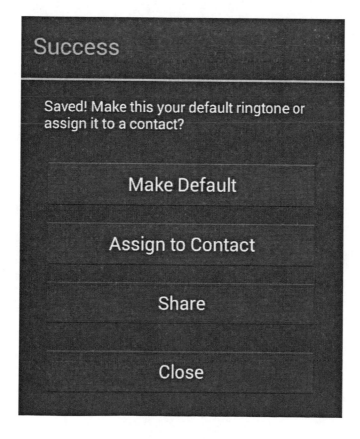

Importing Business Cards Using the Camera

The Galaxy S5 has a very cool feature that allows you to take pictures of business cards and automatically transfer the information to a contact's record. To do so, open the Contacts app, tap the three-dot menu icon, and then "Business cards." Tap the plus sign (+) in the upper-right-hand corner of the screen. The camera will be enabled. Point it at the business card you want to import, hold the camera steady, wait for it to focus, and press the shutter button. The information will be captured. Choose to save the contact to your Google account. Make any necessary corrections to the imported information, and hit "Save."

Merge Accounts

If you don't follow my advice about consolidating all of your contacts in your Google account and come to regret your decision, there's a fairly easy way to catch up. While in the main Contacts view, tap the three-dot menu button and then "Merge Accounts." Click "Google" and all of the contacts in your contact list will be saved to your Google account if they aren't already in it.

> You will find that the contents of the Contacts app have many uses on your Galaxy S5. For example, it is integrated with the Gmail and Messages apps, so that your Galaxy S5 can autofill "To:" fields. It is very helpful and worthwhile to maintain an accurate contact list.

Playing Music

There are many ways to play music on your Galaxy S5. You can stream music from apps like Pandora or Spotify, purchase it from Google Play, import your existing MP3 collection to Google Music, or just copy your existing MP3 files to your Galaxy S5. Let's talk about each option.

Pandora

Pandora is a popular music streaming service that allows you to stream an unlimited amount of music every month for free. However, you don't get to choose every song or artist you listen to. Rather, you create different "stations" based on artists, songs, and genres that you like, and Pandora automatically plays related music it thinks you will like. You can only skip 6 songs per station, per hour.

On one hand, this can be disappointing if you want to be able to pick and choose songs or artists at will, but on the other hand, it can be an amazing way to discover new music. Either way, because it's completely free, you don't have much to lose. The premium version, Pandora One, costs $4.99 per month but eliminates all advertisements and allows more total skips per day.

Download Pandora from the Google Play Store. You'll need an active Internet connection (cellular or Wi-Fi) to use it, so if you have a limited data plan, be careful not to plow through your data allowances.

Spotify

Spotify is another popular music streaming service that gives you more control than Pandora. The free version provides unlimited streaming, and on the mobile app you can listen to any artist's catalog for free on shuffle mode. (That means if you want to only hear one artist, you can, but you can't control the exact songs you hear.) Like Pandora, you get 6 skips per hour and there are advertisements between songs. To remove advertisements and be able to play any song you want, at any time with no skip limit, you must upgrade to Spotify Premium for $9.99 per month. Spotify Premium also has an offline mode, so you can download music to play on the go without using your cellular data.

Download Spotify from the Google Play Store.

Purchasing Music from the Google Play Store

If you prefer purchasing music instead of streaming it, your best option is the Google Play Store. Tracks from the Google Play Store are $1.29, and albums are usually $9.49. For offline listening, you can download purchased tracks to your Galaxy S5 using the Google Play Music app.

However, although songs bought from Google Play belong to you and have no listening limitations, the cost of a single album is nearly the cost of a full month of Spotify Premium, which in my opinion is a much better deal. Keep this in mind before you buy from Google Play.

Importing Your Existing Collection to Google Music

If you already have a large library of MP3 or other audio files on your computer, you can upload up to 20,000 songs to Google Music for free. Those songs can then be streamed or downloaded using the Google Play Music app on your Galaxy S5.

To get started with Google Music, go to the link below on your desktop or laptop, click "Upload music," and then click "Download Music Manager." Install this program and follow its directions to upload your music collection to the cloud. Finally, access it using the Google Play Music app on your Galaxy S5.

> **http://play.google.com/music**

Copying Audio Files Directly to Your Galaxy S5

Finally, if you just want to copy a couple songs or albums from your desktop or laptop to your Galaxy S5, you can simply copy the files over USB and play them using the preloaded "Music" app.

To do so, establish a USB connection with your computer using the directions in Chapter 7. (p. 251) Create a new folder, preferably on your SD card, entitled "Music," and copy your MP3 files directly to it. On many popular desktop music players like iTunes, you can copy your music files simply by dragging them from the program's interface into the appropriate folder on the Galaxy S5. Note that these files may not play on your Galaxy S5 if they were purchased from a music store that uses digital rights management (DRM).

After your files are copied, simply open your Music app and your music will be ready to play.

> The Galaxy S5's music player supports most common file formats, not just MP3s. However, it's a very basic music player. If you're looking for a more full-featured music player, I recommend Play Music, which I discuss in Chapter 9 (p. 280).

Playing Music Using Bluetooth Speakers

To pair your Galaxy S5 with Bluetooth speakers (e.g., Bluetooth headphones or a car stereo), first open the Settings app. Tap "Bluetooth." If Bluetooth is off, turn it on. Put the Bluetooth speakers in pairing/discoverable mode (consult their instruction manual if needed), and wait until the name of the device appears on your Galaxy S5. Tap it and follow the prompts to pair the devices.

Using the Music App's Equalizer

The Music app has a built-in equalizer called SoundAlive. To access it, tap the three-dot menu button in the Music app, tap "Settings," and then "SoundAlive." The interface is a bit unconventional, so try the presets first and then fine-tune as necessary. These settings apply only to the Music app, not to any third-party music players like Pandora, Spotify, or Poweramp.

Customizing Sound Output for Your Ears

The Galaxy S5 has a very interesting and useful feature that performs a mini-hearing test to customize the Galaxy S5's audio output to your ears and headphones. To set it up, plug in the pair of headphones you plan to use with the device, go to a quiet room, and start the process by tapping the Music app's three-dot menu button, "Settings," and then "Adapt Sound."

Note that this process tests your ability to hear different frequencies—not volumes—so listen very carefully and tap "Yes" even if you can only barely hear the beeping. Once you have completed the hearing test, you can specify whether to use the customized settings for calls, music playback, or both, as well as configure your most frequently used ear if you often use only one earbud. Make sure to try the "Preview Adapt Sound" feature to test the results—it makes a big difference for me, and many other users have reported similarly good results.

Unfortunately, for music playback this feature only works with Samsung's stock Music app, so if you use third-party programs, you will not be able to take advantage of Adapt Sound.

Preventing Accidental Battery Drain With Music Auto-Off

It's very easy to accidentally leave music playing on the Galaxy S5—I do it all the time after workouts. With the headphones plugged in, your battery can waste away in vain for hours. To prevent this, enable "Music Auto Off" in the Music app's settings menu. Again, this setting only applies if you are using the Music app to listen to your music.

Exiting the Music App

While the Music app is playing songs, tapping the home button will allow you to multitask while your music continues to play. To exit the app and stop all music playback, pull down the notification panel (p. 54) and tap the "X" next to the persistent Music notification.

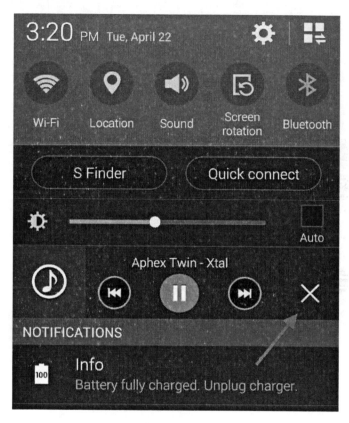

Navigating Using the GPS

Finding and Navigating to Destinations

The Galaxy S5 in conjunction with the Maps app is an excellent co-pilot. You can get directions for driving, walking, bicycling, and public transit, and even use real-time voice and visual navigation. To do so, open the Maps app in your app drawer:

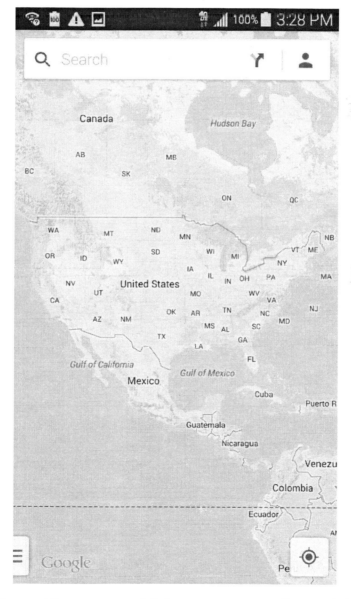

To find locations, addresses, or establishment names, tap the search bar at the top of the screen and type in the name of your destination.

You don't have to enter a specific destination. You can also type in a general search term, like "Italian restaurants," "gas stations," or "ATMs" and Maps will present you with a variety of options.

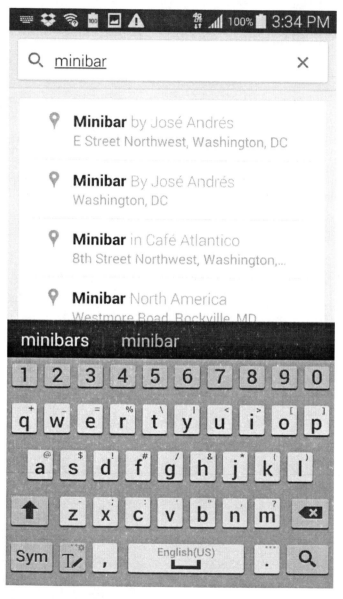

Tap your desired destination from the drop-down list to see your destination on a map.

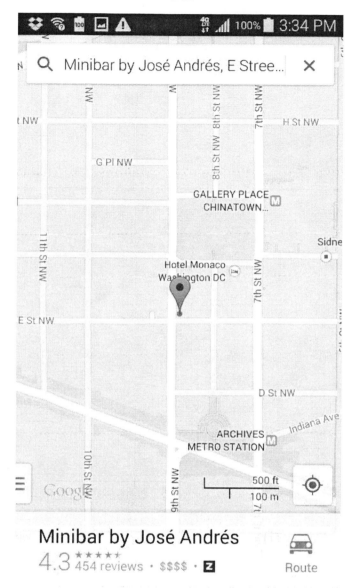

From this screen, tap the "Route" button in the lower-right-hand corner of the screen to get walking, biking, driving, or public transit directions to your destination. Alternatively, swipe the white bottom bar up to see more information about your destination. For example, if you search for a restaurant name as I have, swiping up will show you reviews, hours, and more.

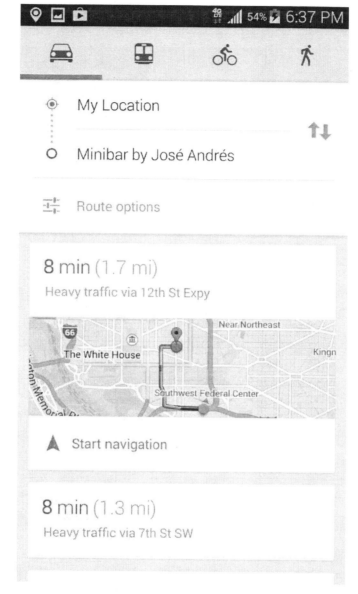

If your location toggle button is turned on in your notification panel, Maps will automatically detect your starting point. Otherwise, you will have to manually enter a landmark or an address. Once you have both a starting and an ending point, Maps will present you with two to three different route options.

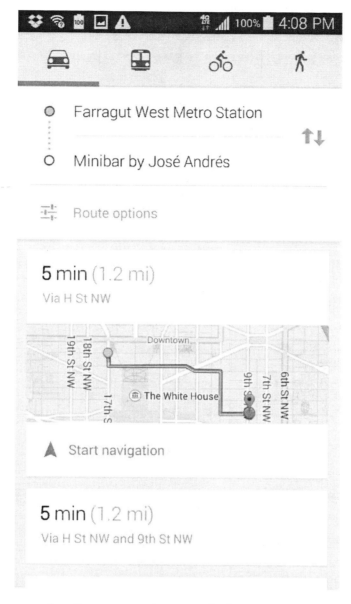

To change your mode of transportation, use the buttons at the top of the screen. Then, tap on one of the routes to see it plotted on a map. In the screenshot below, I have tapped on the first one (5 min via H St NW):

To start voice-guided turn-by-turn navigation, tap the "Start" button in the lower-right-hand corner of the screen. Your Galaxy S5 will speak directions and show you a detailed map guiding you to your destination.

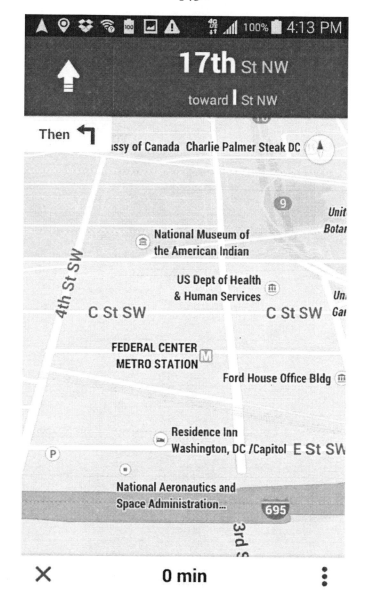

Now that you know how to use the Maps app to find destinations and navigate to them, let's discuss the other controls in the Maps app.

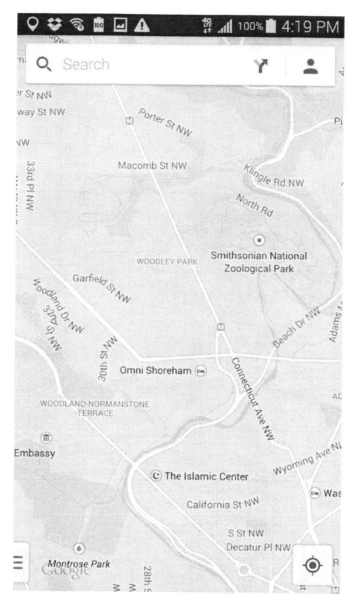

While viewing a map like the one above, you can pinch with two fingers to zoom or use one finger to pan around the map. Type destinations into the Search bar as described above, or, once you've entered a search term, tap the list icon on the right side of the search bar to view more results:

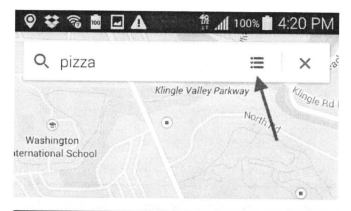

Results List

Italian Pizza Kitchen

3.9 ★★★★★ 13 reviews • $

Standard Italian comfort food &
big TVs

3.5 mi • 11:00 AM - 11:00 PM

Sorriso Restaurant

4.0 ★★★★★ 105 reviews • $$

Casual Italian place with
homestyle fare

4.4 mi • 5:30 PM - 9:30 PM

Z Best Restaurants Near the National Zoo...

Pizzeria Paradiso

3.9 ★★★★★ 728 reviews • $$

Wood-fired pizzeria with vast beer
list

2.5 mi • 11:30 AM - 11:00 PM

Pines of Florence

Tap the 'head and shoulders' icon in the upper-right-hand corner of the screen to view information about you, such as your home and work addresses, your saved places, and your recent places. Tap the compass icon in the bottom-right-hand corner of the screen to make the map jump to your present location. Tap the small tab in the lower-left-hand corner of the screen or swipe right from the left edge of the screen to reveal this menu:

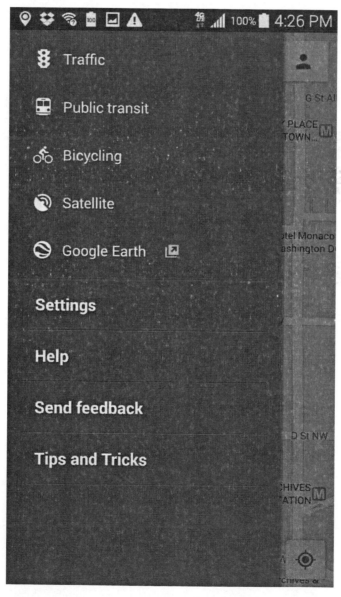

Using this menu, you can enable or disable various map layers such as current traffic conditions, public transit, bicycle paths, and more.

Showing Current Traffic Conditions

Google collects real-time, live traffic data from DOT sensors installed in roads as well as from other Android users' phones. You can easily overlay this information on a map. To do so, open the toolbar as shown above and tap "Traffic." (Green = clear, yellow = some traffic, red = congested.) You'll find this data is very accurate and up-to-date!

Setting Your Home and Work Locations for Easy Directions

Set your home and work addresses by opening the menu, tapping "Settings," and then "Edit Home or Work." By doing so, you will be able to simply type "home" or "work" as starting or ending points when getting directions, rather than typing out your entire address. This is also important for Google Now (p. 166) to function optimally.

Improving Your Location Precision

To find your current location, Maps uses a combination of GPS, cellular, and Wi-Fi data. To make sure you're allowing Maps to take full advantage of these resources, open the menu, tap "Settings," and then "Location accuracy tips." Follow any instructions that it gives you. This is particularly useful if you spend a lot of time indoors, because GPS is a line-of-sight technology and is not available in many buildings.

As long as you allowed full location access when first configuring your Galaxy S5, your location accuracy should already be optimized. If this is the case, you will receive a message notifying you of that, and you will not need to make any changes to your location settings.

Saving Maps for Offline Use

Google used to make it easy to save maps for offline use, but removed this setting in recent versions of Maps, presumably because they want you to be connected to the Internet as much as possible. Still, there are times when that won't be possible. Fortunately, there is a trick to save maps offline. Pull up the location you're interested in and type "OK Maps" into the search box, and hit enter. Maps will save the current screen for offline use. Note that depending on how far you are zoomed out, it may only save major streets, so zoom and repeat the process as necessary depending on how much detail you need.

Using the Calendar

Samsung includes a custom Calendar app, which I think is better than Google Calendar (available on the Google Play Store and "pure" Android devices (p. 33) but not included on the Galaxy S5). Its tabbed interface is very user-friendly and the layout is intuitive. You'll find the Calendar in your app drawer.

Navigating the Interface

Upon opening Calendar, you will see a Month and Agenda view.

To switch to Year, Month without Agenda, Week, Day, or Agenda-Only view, tap the word "Month" in the upper-left-hand corner of the screen and select your desired view:

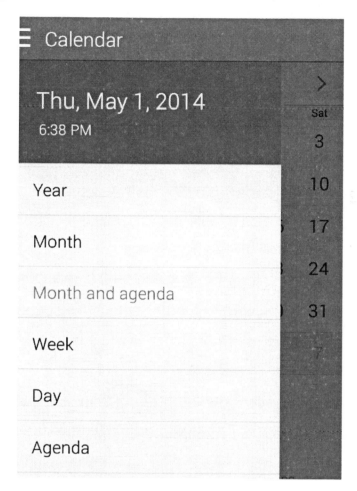

Personally, I find Week view to be the most useful view, although Month and Day are often useful for "zooming" in or out of my schedule. Year does not display any events, and is mostly only useful for determining the day of the week for a specific date, or tapping a month to jump to it in the Month display. Agenda displays your upcoming events in a sequential, text-based list.

> The Calendar app automatically synchronizes with your Google account, which means that if you log into your Gmail account on your desktop or laptop computer and pull up the calendar, you will see all of the events that are in your Galaxy S5's Calendar App.

Creating a New Event

To create a new event, tap the plus sign in the upper-right-hand corner of the screen. If you see a warning saying that Google Calendar cannot sync with Samsung Kies, just check "Do not show again" and dismiss the notification.

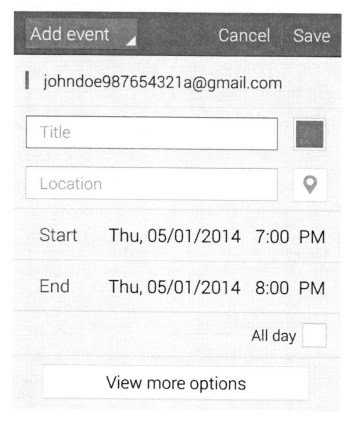

- **Add event**: Tap to change the record from an event to a task. More about tasks below.

- **(Your email address)**: Tap to change the calendar to which your event will be saved. Useful if you have multiple Google calendars to separate personal and work tasks, etc. If you don't have multiple calendars but want to set them up, log into your Gmail account on your desktop or laptop computer, and access your Calendar. Look for the "My calendars" box on the left-hand side of the screen, click the down arrow, and then "Create new calendar." Any new calendars you create will automatically be synced to your Galaxy S5's Calendar app.

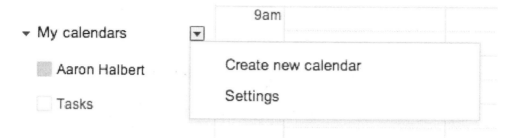

- **Title**: Color-code the event and give it a name.

- **Location**: Enter a location name, or tap the button to the right to select a location using the Maps app.

- **Start/End**: Specify the starting and ending times/dates for the event.

- **All Day**: Do not give the event any specific timeframe. Note that you can have other events overlapping with all day events.

- **View more options**: Set up a popup or email reminder (alarm) for the event, add contacts from your Contacts list as attendees, assign a sticker to the event for easier identification, and more. Note that the "Show me as" and "Privacy" options are only relevant if your Google calendar is shared with other people.

Fill out the necessary information and then tap "Save."

Creating a New Task/To-Do Item

To add a new task instead of an event, create a new event, then tap the "Add event" button and change it to "Add task."

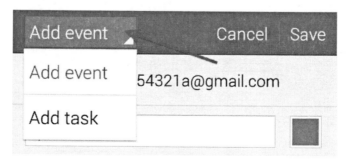

Enter information such as the title due date, and reminder as you would for a regular calendar event.

Tasks will appear on your calendar along with scheduled events, but unlike events, have a checkbox so you can easily mark them as complete.

Unfortunately, there is no way to synchronize tasks in the Calendar app with Google Tasks. If you frequently use the task list in your Gmail account and want to sync it with your Galaxy S5, I highly recommend the third-party GTasks app. I discuss GTasks in <u>Chapter 9</u> (p. 280).

Managing Events and Tasks

To manage existing calendar events or tasks, tap them once in Week or Day mode. This will bring you to detail view.

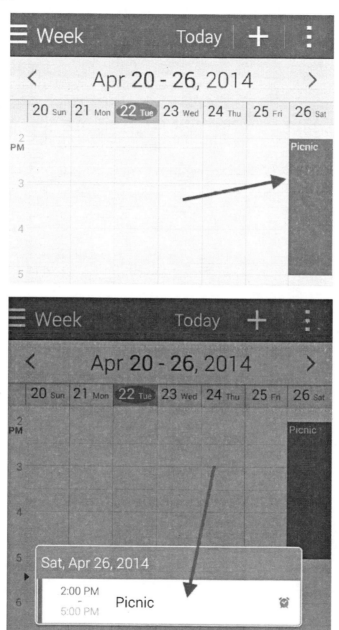

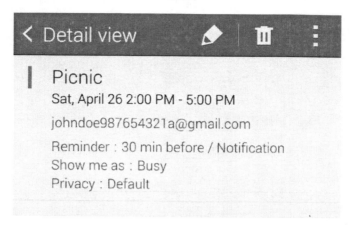

Tap the pencil icon to edit the event details, or the trashcan icon to delete it. To copy the event, tap the three-dot menu button and then "Copy." You can also share the event by tapping "Share via" in the menu.

Installing and Uninstalling Apps

One of the great benefits of the Android OS is the ability to install third-party apps to add functionality to your device. For example, I have apps for my bank, for Amazon and eBay, for reading RSS news feeds, and more.

Installing Apps

The best and only official source for new apps is the Google Play Store. You will find it in your app drawer as the shortcut named "Play Store."

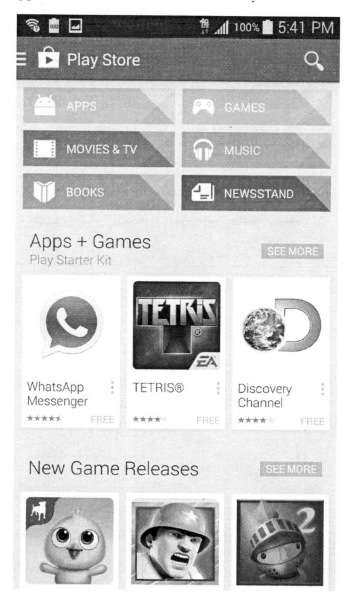

Tap the magnifying glass in the upper-right-hand corner of the screen to search for and install new apps. If you know the name of the app you want, enter it, or otherwise use search terms to find what you want (e.g., "shopping list").

Protecting Yourself From Malware and Viruses

The Google Play Store now contains more than one million apps, and some of these contain malware and viruses. There are several ways to protect yourself against these threats.

- First, only install apps that you have found via trusted publications. For example, apps reviewed on blogs like AndroidCentral.com can be trusted. Also, the apps I discuss in Chapter 9 (p. 280) are completely tested and safe. If you want a shopping list app, run a Google search for "Android shopping list app" and find apps that are well-reviewed and frequently discussed. A little bit of research can help you steer clear of sketchy options.

- Second, do not download pirated apps. Not only is it illegal to do so, but pirated apps frequently contain malware and viruses, even if it's a trustworthy title.

- Third, pay attention to the number of downloads an app has in the Play Store. In general, apps with hundreds of thousands of downloads or more have probably been vetted thoroughly enough to be safe. This is not a guarantee, however, and many apps with fewer downloads are perfectly legitimate. It is only one of many possible signs.

- Fourth, pay attention to the permissions that an app requires. You will see this information every time you initiate an app installation. Do they make sense, given the program's function? For example, if you are downloading a flashlight app that requests full network access, it would be very suspect. I always try to download apps that require minimal permissions, and permissions that make sense for what the app is supposed to do.

- Fifth, you use antivirus software such as Lookout, which comes preinstalled on most Galaxy S5s.

Branching Out From the Play Store

Although the Google Play Store is the largest and most common source of new apps, it is not the only one. For example, Amazon has its own app store, which must be downloaded directly from Amazon's website. (Unsurprisingly, Google is not willing to allow a competing app store on the Google Play Store.)

> **http://www.amazon.com/gp/mas/get/android**

When you install software from outside the Play Store (such as the Amazon App Store), there are more warnings than usual. Here is an example:

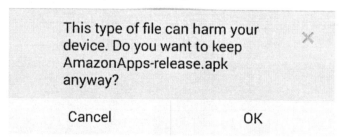

Here, I have clicked on the "Download the Amazon Appstore" button. Chrome has begun to download the .APK file, and has warned me about downloading apps from outside the Google Play Store. Since I trust Amazon, I will tap "OK."

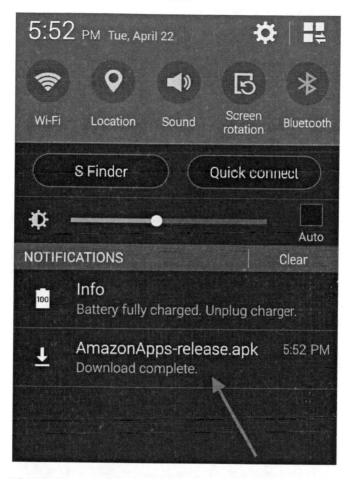

After tapping "OK," I have swiped down the <u>notification panel</u> (p. 54). I will tap on the download notification to install the .APK file.

Because I have Lookout anti-virus installed, I can scan the file before installing it. I will select "Scan with Lookout before install" and then tap "Just once."

Here, I will tap "Settings" to allow my Galaxy S5 to temporarily allow installation of an application not downloaded from the Google Play Store.

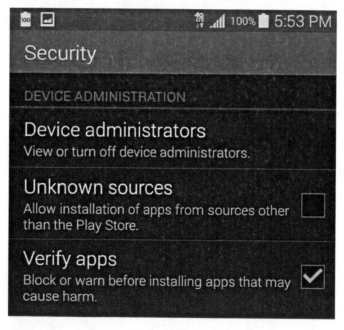

I will check "Unknown sources" to allow installation to continue.

Here, I will tap "OK" to allow installation to continue. If you do not want to see this notification again in the future, uncheck the "Allow initial installation only" box.

Finally, on the following screen, I will tap "Next" and then "Install" to finish installing the Amazon App Store.

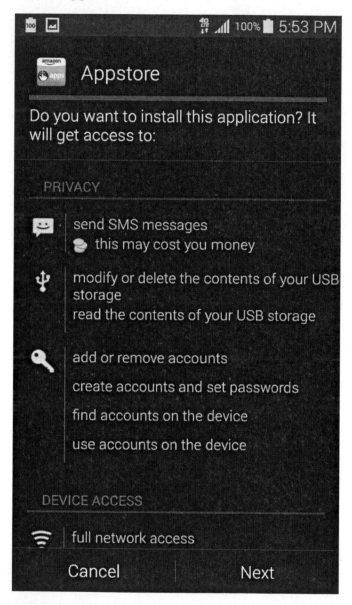

The Amazon App Store is now available in my app drawer. Any other apps you install from a source other than the Google Play Store will require a similar process.

It is possible to download and install Android apps directly from the Internet. To do so, download the file and then tap the notification in your notification panel. These files will have a .APK file extension and are installed using the same method shown above.

Uninstalling Apps

To uninstall an app, first go to your app drawer (*not* a home screen, which will only remove the shortcut). Tap and hold on the app's icon, drag it up to the "Remove" area, and release. Here, I am uninstalling Spotify.

Tap "OK" on the confirmation dialog box to complete uninstallation.

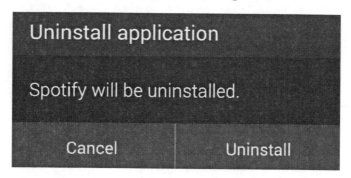

Getting a Refund and Trying Paid Apps for Free

The Google Play Store has a 15-minute grace period for all purchased apps. If you decide you don't want the app within 15 minutes of buying it, go back to its page in the Play Store and tap the "Refund" button. This is a great way to evaluate paid apps as long as you're fast about it.

Google Now

What Is Google Now?

Google Now is Google's answer to Apple's Siri—a personal assistant that intelligently interprets your voice commands. However, Google Now also includes a proactive approach to information delivery through its **card** system, something that Siri lacks. Using the card system, Google Now delivers notifications to you throughout the day that it thinks will be useful, such as traffic information, flight information, nearby events, and so on. Google Now accomplishes this by accessing personal information such as your Gmail inbox, your Google web history, and your location history. The more you use Google Now, the more it learns about you and the smarter it gets.

> Start Google Now by tapping and holding the Galaxy S5's home button.

In total, Google Now has 39 different cards:

- Boarding Pass

- Activity Summary

- Next Appointment

- Traffic & Transit

- Flights

- Weather

- Restaurant Reservations

- Events

- Hotels

- Friends' Birthdays

- Your Birthday

- Packages

- Location Reminders

- Event Reminders

- Sports

- Movies

- Time Reminders

- Concerts

- Stocks

- Zillow (apartment & real estate finder)

- Developing Story & Breaking News

- Research Topic

- New Books

- Fandango

- New Video Games

- Public Alerts

- Nearby Events

- New Albums

- Places

- Translation

- Public Transit

- Nearby Photo Spots

- Nearby Attractions

- News Topic

- Currency

- Time At Home

- New TV Episodes

- Website Update

- What To Watch

> In previous versions of Google Now, it was possible to toggle individual cards on and off. Google has since removed this functionality to encourage users allow Google Now to automate the process. So, you will see these cards come and go as Google Now learns about your information needs.

In summary, Google Now performs two main functions: (1) **proactive** information delivery through the card system (information it thinks will be helpful, but that you do not directly request), and (2) **reactive** information delivery through the voice command system (information that you directly request). If you think about it, this is exactly what you'd want from a personal assistant—things done at your request, or anticipated ahead of time.

Setting up Google Now

The first time you start Google Now, you will see this screen:

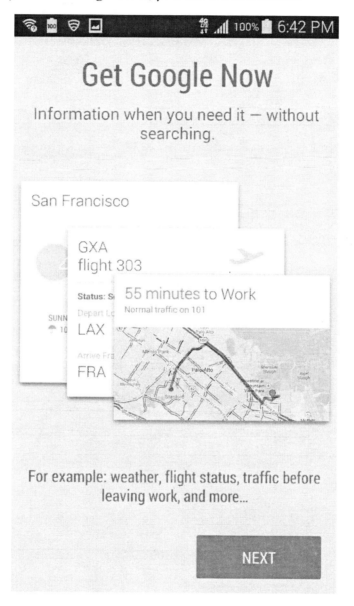

Tap "Next," and then "Yes, I'm in" to enable Google Now. From now on, anytime you tap and hold the home button, you will be taken straight to Google Now's home screen:

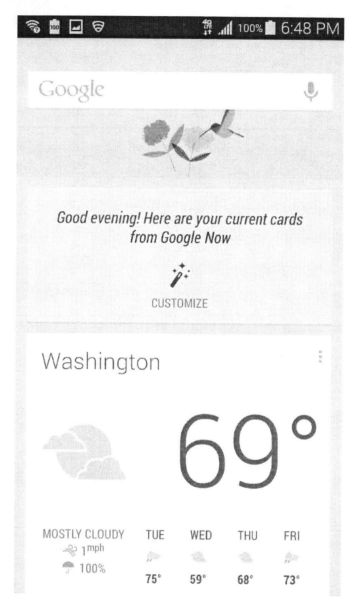

You can also initiate Google Now voice commands from the Galaxy S5's home screen as long as you do not remove the Google Now widget that comes on the home screen by default. As long as you have this widget, just say "OK Google" while on the home screen to prepare it for a voice command.

If you removed the Google Now widget, see <u>this section</u> (p. 52) for more information on re-adding it.

I'll come back the Google Now home screen in a moment—but first, there are a few settings you need to change to make sure you get the most out of Google Now.

- First, make sure Web History is turned on, so that Google Now can learn your information needs from your Google searches. To do this, tap and hold the recent key to access Google Now's menu, go to Settings → Accounts & Privacy and turn the Web History slider on.

- Second, make sure that location reporting is on. Tap "Google location settings" above the Web History slider, then gap "Google Location Reporting," and make sure both Location Reporting and Location History are on.

- Third, enable contact recognition to allow Google Now to access your Galaxy S5's contact list. Tap and hold the recent button to go to Google Now's menu → Settings → Accounts & Privacy and enable "Contact recognition."

- Fourth, exit Google Now and open the Maps app. Go to Maps' settings → "Edit home or work" and set your home and work addresses.

- Finally, swipe to the bottom of Google Now's home screen and tap the magic wand icon. Tell it how you usually travel, and tap through the other available settings, answering questions like your favorite sports teams and TV provider. This information will help Google Now get up to speed.

Now, you are ready to start using Google Now.

Using Google Now's Card/Notification System

At first, you will only have a few general cards such as current weather and nearby places. The longer you have Google Now enabled, though, the more it will learn about you. It will start to show you more specialized cards and send more relevant notifications to your notification panel. In my experience, it takes about one to two weeks for Google Now to really kick into gear.

Even if you don't proactively ask Google Now questions, it will still monitor your data in the background and learn about your information needs. For example, if you receive emails with flight reservations or package tracking numbers, Google Now will send you flight reminders and updates and track your packages automatically. It will also monitor your calendar and remind you about upcoming events.

However, if you do ask Google Now a lot of questions, it will learn even more about you. For example, if you run a few searches for your favorite sports team's scores, you will soon receive a new card with your team's scores.

If you want to stop receiving a certain type of notification—for example, sports scores—open Google Now, find the relevant card, and swipe it away:

Alternatively, tap the three vertical dots in its upper-right-hand corner of the card and tell Google Now you are no longer interested:

Dismissing cards will not permanently remove them the first time—it will only hide them until the next time they are updated. But, if you keep swiping away a certain card, Google Now will eventually learn you don't need it, and it won't appear again.

Using Google Now's Voice Command System

Now, let's talk a bit about the **voice command system**, the other function of Google Now.

To prepare Google Now for a voice command, say "OK, Google" out loud anywhere in Google Now (except the menu), or on the Galaxy S5's home screen (as long as you have the Google Now widget, as I mentioned earlier). You will see a red microphone, indicating you can proceed with your command or inquiry:

Below are the results of a couple inquiries I spoke to Google Now, to give you an idea of the types of information it can provide.

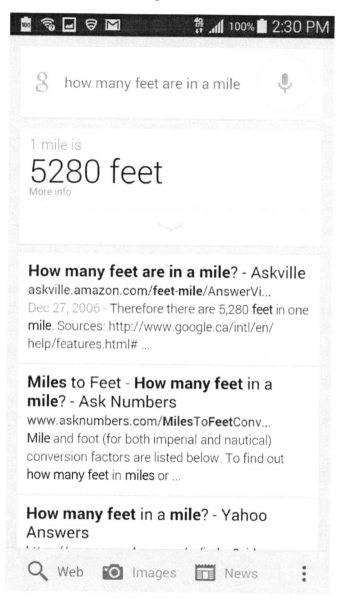

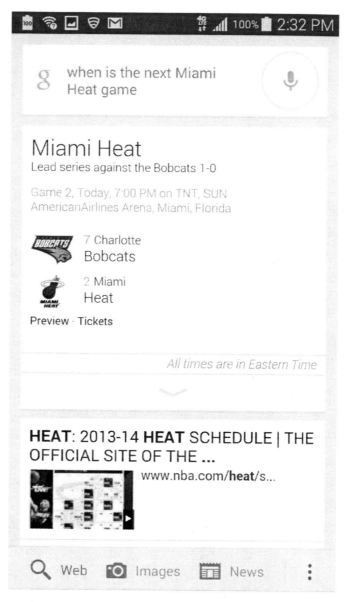

Here is a list of voice commands for you to try. Google is always adding more capabilities, so even if you don't see something on this list, try it.

- "Set an alarm for seven A.M."

- "Schedule a meeting at 9 A.M. Thursday morning with John from Microsoft."

- "Will it rain tomorrow?"

- "How many Japanese yen are in three hundred U.S. dollars?"

- "Remind me to buy laundry detergent the next time I'm at Safeway."

- "Send a text message to Craig Johnston saying hello."

- "Driving directions to the nearest Safeway."

- "Call Target."

- "What time is it in London?"

- "Navigate to Yellowstone National Park."

- "Open (app name)."

- "Play (song name)."

- "What's this song?" (Google Now will listen through the microphone)

- "Show all hotels near me."

For a full list of voice commands that is updated on a regular basis, check out this discussion thread on XDA:

> **http://forum.xda-developers.com/showthread.php?t=1961636**
>
> **(Short URL: http://goo.gl/xTXDpl)**

Sharing Your Commute

Remember Google Latitude, the web app that allowed you to share your location with your friends? Google Now has a similar feature built in that will automatically share the details of your commute with friends or family. If this sounds like a good idea to you—and I won't blame you if it doesn't—you can enable it by holding the recent button, tapping "Settings," going to the "Accounts & Privacy" menu, and enabling Commute Sharing. Make sure to specify who you want to share your commute with. They will then receive a card on their Google Now home screen containing your commute information.

Privacy Concerns

Using Google Now requires a great deal of trust on your part, because it requires access to so much personal data. My position, however, is that you might as well trust Google. I'm not necessarily saying Google is benevolent—just that their interest is in making money, not being Big Brother. Obviously, each user has to make his or her own decision, and enabling Google Now will allow Google to track and centralize a lot more information about you. Personally, I've made the decision to not worry about it.

Disabling Google Now

If you've had enough of Google Now and want to disable it, pull up the menu, go to "Settings," and turn off the Google Now slider. Be warned that this will reset all features including cards you've accumulated.

S Voice: A Worthy Competitor

Samsung packages the Galaxy S5 with its own competitor to Google Now called S Voice. It has most, if not all of the voice command features of Google Now, without the card system. Its voice recognition is surprisingly good—often better than Google Now's, albeit somewhat slower—so I suggest you try these commands in it as well. You might find that S Voice is actually a better solution for you than Google Now, especially if you don't care for the card system. In the long run, I expect Google Now to outpace S Voice because, well, it has the support of Google. But in the meantime, S Voice is no slouch. Open S Voice by tapping the home button twice.

> There's at least one major caveat with S Voice: it can't handle any commands at all related to email (including the Gmail app). If this is important to you, Google Now is a better option.

The Share Via Tool

You'll see the Share Via tool in nearly every app on the Galaxy S5, so you need to understand what it does. The Share Via tool looks like a map route:

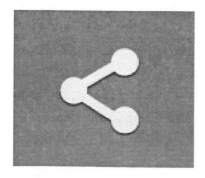

Tapping this icon in any app allows you to send content to other apps. For example, in the following screenshot I am viewing a photo in the Gallery app. Tapping the Share Via button gives me numerous options:

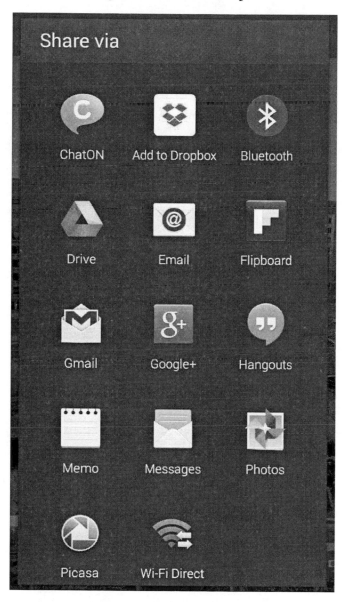

I can upload the photo to Dropbox, send it as an email attachment, send it as a picture message, and so on.

As I said, you'll see this tool all over the place on you know what it is. If you need to get a file from one app to another, chances are the Share Via tool is what you need.

Chapter 6: Intermediate Functions – Useful Tips & Tricks

Congratulations! By now, you should be getting quite comfortable with your Galaxy S5. You've learned how to perform all the basic functions on the device. Now we'll start to discuss intermediate-level tips and tricks.

Multitasking With Multi Window

Multi Window allows you to open two apps at the same time, in either portrait or landscape mode:

To enable Multi Window, swipe the notification panel down with two fingers to call up the <u>extended toggle buttons</u> (p. 56). Tap Multi Window to enable it. After you have done so, you will see a small icon appear on the edge of your screen. Tapping this icon will pull up the Multi Window control panel, from which you can launch apps to be used in Multi Window mode. You can also tap, hold, and drag this icon to move the control panel to the right edge of the screen.

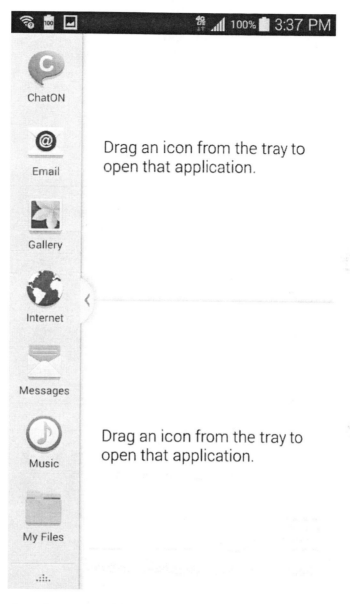

Multi Window is only compatible with certain apps—and not even all of those preloaded on the Galaxy S5. However, there is a third-party app called MultiWindow Apps Manager that lets you add any app you want to your Multi Window menu. It requires your Galaxy S5 to be rooted. See the sections on rooting your Galaxy S5 (p. 255) and improving Multi Window (p. 267).

Once enabled, you can show and hide the Multi Window control panel by tapping and holding the back button for about two seconds.

From the Multi Window settings menu (accessible via system settings), you can also toggle the setting "Open in multi window view." When this option is selected, the Galaxy S5 will default to a Multi Window view whenever you open files from within the My Files file manager or the Video app, as well as email attachments in the Email app and text message attachments in the Messages app. This feature does not work in other apps such as Gmail or third-party text messaging apps.

In action, it looks like this:

A final feature to note is that you can scroll all the way down the Multi Window toolbar and tap the tiny up arrow to edit the applications shown in the main panel, or create a new shortcut.

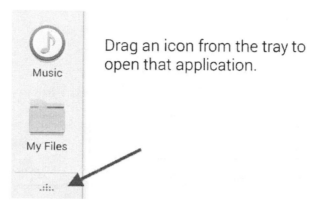

Drag an icon from the tray to open that application.

Use the latter option when you already have two screens on the window, and a new dual shortcut will be created that opens both of those apps at the same time. For example, here I have created a dual shortcut for Gmail and Chrome:

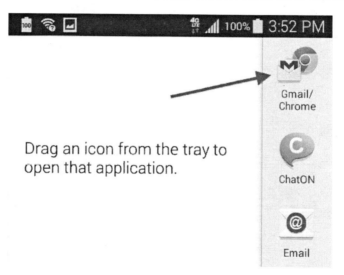

Drag an icon from the tray to open that application.

Securing Your Data

Setting Up a Lock Screen

As I noted earlier in this book, Android's lock screen is what keeps your Galaxy S5 safe from unauthorized access. When enabled, your Galaxy S5 will lock itself after a specified duration when it's asleep. In this way, if you lose your Galaxy S5, no one will be able to use it or access your data without proper authorization.

To set up a lock screen, go to system settings → Lock Screen. There are multiple locking methods available, including:

- **Swipe**: This is a zero-security option that is only useful for preventing the device from being accidentally operated in your pocket (although if the screen were receiving random input, it would not be hard to accidentally dismiss the lock screen as well). On the Galaxy S4, the swipe lock screen allowed you to add widgets to it, but this feature has been removed on the Galaxy S5. I strongly suggest you avoid the swipe setting. You probably have a great deal of sensitive information on your Galaxy S5, and if you do not have security measures in place, you will open yourself up to identity theft and other crimes should you lose your Galaxy S5. Using a lock screen with a fingerprint, PIN, password, or other feature is worth the minor inconvenience of having to enter it when you power on your Galaxy S5.

- **Pattern**: This option allows you to unlock your Galaxy S5 by drawing a pattern on a 3x3 grid (with a PIN backup). Pattern unlock is more secure than signature unlock, but I still suggest a PIN or password instead. It is sometimes possible for thieves to defeat pattern security by retracing smudges on the screen.

- **Fingerprint**: Fingerprint is a new feature on the Galaxy S5. The Galaxy S5's home button doubles as a fingerprint reader, and this option allows you to unlock your device with a simple swipe of your finger. Personally, this is the option I use. I formerly preferred PIN security but fingerprint recognition is fast, accurate, and quite secure.

- **PIN**: This unlock option secures your lock screen with a minimum 4-digit numerical PIN code. There is no maximum PIN length. A PIN is much faster and easier to type than a password on a keyboard, especially when using one hand. Before I got the Galaxy S5, I used a six-digit PIN code on my Android devices.

- **Password**: A password works almost exactly like a PIN, but can include letters and special characters in addition to numbers. A password is more secure than a PIN code but slower and more difficult to type each time you wake your Galaxy S5. I suggest only using a password unlock option if your data is extremely sensitive.

- **None**: The final option in this menu is to use no lock screen whatsoever. Although this setting is convenient, I suggest carefully thinking through the consequences of losing your phone before using it.

In addition to choosing a locking method, I suggest putting a "Reward If Found" message in the "Owner Information" field (available in the Lock Screen system menu), with a phone number to call. This information will be prominently displayed on your lock screen. Also, make sure to set the locking delay and choose whether to lock instantly with the power key. Personally, I set a 5 second delay without power key locking. That way, if I accidentally hit the power button, I can turn my Galaxy S5 on again without having to swipe my finger.

Encrypting Your Galaxy S5

If you have extremely sensitive data on your Galaxy S5 (for example, so sensitive that attackers would be willing to physically extract the memory chip to bypass your lock screen), consider encrypting your Galaxy S5. To do so, go to system settings → Security. Encrypt both the device and your external SD card. This process may take 1-2 hours, so make sure to plug in your Galaxy S5 first. With your information encrypted, even a computer forensics laboratory will be unable to read information on your Galaxy S5 without your authorization.

Locating, Locking, and Remotely Wiping Your Galaxy S5

Google offers a convenient and free remote locate/erase service. To use these features, you'll first need to ensure your location services are enabled and set to "High accuracy" in system settings → Location.

> This feature works well and is totally free. However, I personally use a third-party security app called Cerberus that has more options. Cerberus requires a one-time fee of a few dollars, but in my opinion it is well worth it. Read about it <u>here</u> (p. 283).

To locate your Galaxy S5, login to your Gmail account, go to the link below on your desktop PC, click the gear icon in the upper-right-hand corner of the screen, and click "Android Device Manager."

https://play.google.com/store

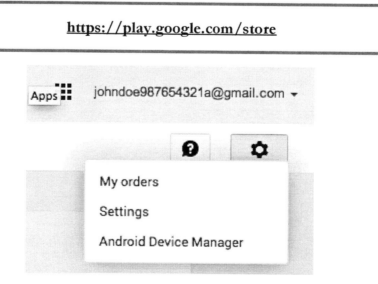

Google will automatically locate your Galaxy S5 if possible, and report its location within a few seconds.

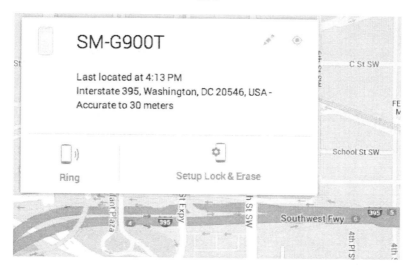

As you can see, Google can locate your Galaxy S5 very precisely using a combination of GPS, cellular, and Wi-Fi signals. Tap "Ring" to have the Galaxy S5 ring at full volume for 5 minutes to help you find your Galaxy S5.

In the unfortunate event that your Galaxy S5 is stolen and not simply lost, you may want to remotely lock and/or wipe the device. Note that you must set up this functionality ahead of time, or you'll be out of luck when you need it.

To initiate setup, first locate your Galaxy S5 as described above, and then click "Setup Lock & Erase." You will be prompted to send a notification to your Galaxy S5, which will pop up in the notification panel. Tap the notification and you'll be prompted to activate the feature. Do so.

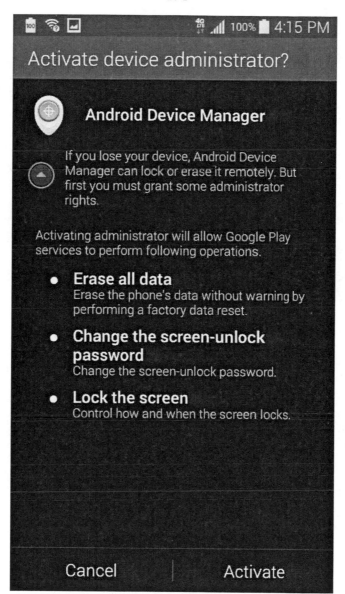

After tapping "Activate," you'll be taken to this settings screen:

Leave both boxes checked and tap the back button to save your settings. From now on, when you access the Android Device Manager using your desktop PC, you will see these options:

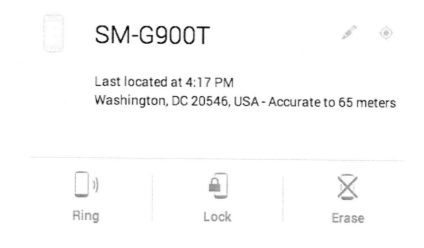

If you lose your Galaxy S5 and you haven't set up this feature in advance, you're in trouble. There used to be a popular app called Plan B that you could remotely install on a lost phone, but it is not compatible with newer Android devices. The moral of the story? Prepare ahead of time.

Attaching Any File You Want to a Gmail Message

In the past, Google only allowed you to attach photos or videos to Gmail messages. Although Gmail attachments have been improved a lot since then, Gmail's attachment tool still doesn't give you access to all the directories on your Galaxy S5. A file browser like ES File Explorer, discussed in Chapter 9 (p. 280), allows you to bypass this limitation.

To attach any file to a Gmail message, open ES File Explorer and tap and hold to select the file you wish to attach. Tap "More."

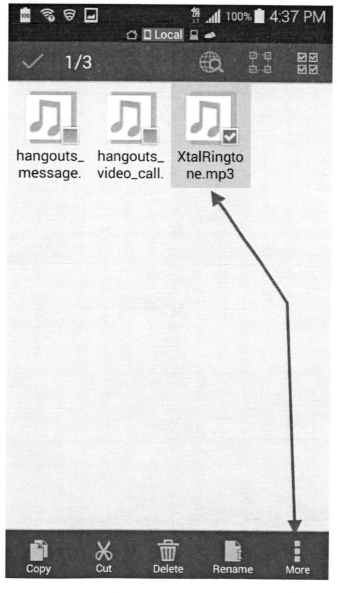

Next, tap "Share" and share via Gmail.

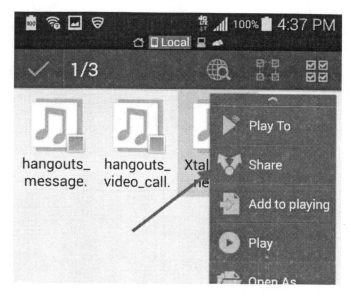

You will then see a new Gmail message with your file attached.

S Beam, Android Beam, Wi-Fi Direct, DLNA, NFC, WTF?!?

The Galaxy S5 includes a huge variety of wireless features, and it can be very hard to disentangle them. Each of these protocols is something slightly different, so what exactly does each one do?

Let's start with NFC. NFC stands for "Near-Field Communications," and is a fairly new feature in Android smartphones. NFC is basically synonymous with RFID technology. Sorry to introduce yet another acronym! RFID tags are tiny chips that can store information but do not require batteries. They are frequently used for inventory tracking in stores, subway passes, and in tap-to-pay debit and credit cards. So how does the Galaxy S5 use its NFC chip?

The first way is through the protocol called "Android Beam," found under the NFC menu in system settings. It is used for sending links, images, contacts, and other content to and from other Android devices that have Android Beam. Data transfer is not actually accomplished through NFC, though—rather, the NFC chips 'handshake' with each other, establishing a Bluetooth connection between the two Android Beam-enabled devices.

In general, you can expect Android Beam to work with stock apps such as the Gallery, Internet, Contacts, and Music. To use it, enable Android Beam, open the song/contact/photo/etc. you wish to share, and place both devices back-to-back. When prompted, tap the content you wish to share and then pull the devices apart to initiate data transfer.

The Galaxy S5 also uses NFC technology to read and write NFC tags, which can automate software actions in conjunction with the Samsung TecTiles app (p. 268). Additionally, with the Google Wallet (p. 213) app, you can use your Galaxy S5's NFC chip at tap-to-pay terminals.

So now you understand the relationship between NFC and Android Beam. What about S Beam? S Beam is a Samsung-only feature that sounds quite similar to Android Beam, and in fact, it does exactly the same thing as Android Beam. But whereas Android Beam uses NFC to 'handshake' for a Bluetooth connection, S Beam 'handshakes' to establish a Wi-Fi Direct connection to send files much faster.

To send files with S Beam, make sure it is turned on for both devices in system settings → NFC, and then follow the exact same steps described above for Android Beam.

To summarize, S Beam is a strictly better version of Android Beam, but it only works between two newer Samsung devices.

OK, so if S Beam uses NFC to create a Wi-Fi Direct connection, why is there a separate Wi-Fi Direct option in the Wi-Fi settings (system settings → Wi-Fi)? This option lets you directly pair two devices that support Wi-Fi Direct, whether they are Samsung devices or not. You lose the convenience of the automatic NFC handshake, but you gain the ability to transfer data to any Android phone with Wi-Fi Direct. Additionally, with Wi-Fi Direct you can send any file you want using the Share Via tool (p. 180) in My Files, ES File Explorer, or another file browser, which is not true of S Beam.

To use this feature, open both devices to their respective Wi-Fi Direct settings pages (again, on the Galaxy S5 go to system settings → Wi-Fi → three-dot menu) and tap on the other device's name under "Available Devices." After successfully pairing the devices, use any app's Share Via tool to share a file via Wi-Fi Direct.

However, there is a catch to all of this. There is a third-party program available called SuperBeam (p. 293) (free on the Google Play Store) that is by far the easiest way to send files between Android devices using Wi-Fi. It can send any file to any device—Samsung or not—and doesn't even require the devices to have Wi-Fi Direct support in their operating systems. It is an example of how third-party developers can sometimes solve problems better than the big companies.

I strongly encourage you to use SuperBeam instead of Android Beam, S Beam, or the built-in Wi-Fi Direct feature to send big files between Android devices. It really simplifies things.

Finally, DLNA is a protocol for streaming videos, photos, and music to and from your Galaxy S5 over Wi-Fi. If you use this feature to share with other Android devices that support DLNA, you will find that your videos, photos, and/or music appear in the other person's Music, and Video apps. Similarly, their media will appear in your apps if they have enabled sharing on their device.

In order for DLNA to function, both devices must be connected to the same Wi-Fi network. Go to system settings → Nearby Devices. Turn this feature on and select the type of content you wish to share. You will then be able to access files on your Galaxy S5 from other DLNA devices. To stream the other direction, open the Music or Video apps and search for nearby devices. Open them, and you'll be able to access their media as well.

Pairing With Bluetooth Devices Such as a Headset or Car Stereo

Whereas Wi-Fi is used to connect to the Internet through wireless networks, Bluetooth is most commonly used for connecting to car stereos, headsets, keyboards & mice, or other mobile devices. Connecting to a Bluetooth device is called "pairing." To pair a device with your Galaxy S5, make sure Bluetooth is turned on in the notification panel, and then go to system settings → Bluetooth.

From this screen, first turn on Bluetooth using the button in the upper-right-hand corner of the screen. Then, tap on your device's name to make it discoverable, which is necessary if you wish to pair it with any other Bluetooth device. Doing so will make it discoverable for only 2 minutes, in order to prevent unauthorized devices from attempting to access your Galaxy S5. You will also need to make the other device discoverable (may be called "pairing mode" or something similar); consult its instruction manual for details.

After you have made both devices discoverable, tap the "Scan" button and wait for the other device to appear under "Available Devices." Once it has, tap on it and follow the prompts to pair the devices. You will probably have to confirm a PIN code on both devices to establish a connection.

Setting Up a Wi-Fi Hotspot and Tethering Your Computer

The Galaxy S5's tethering/hotspot feature allows you to share your cellular Internet connection with another device, such as a laptop, a desktop, or even another Android device. It makes your Galaxy S5 act as a wireless router.

Note that your hotspot feature may fail to work if you do not pay for it; all major U.S. carriers bill wireless hotspots as an add-on that generally runs between $20-30 per month.

To turn on the hotspot, go to system settings → Tethering and Mobile HotSpot. Depending on your carrier, this option may have a slightly different name but will still be found in system settings or app drawer.

Upon enabling your hotspot, you will be prompted to enter a name (SSID) for your network, select a security protocol (choose WPA2 PSK), and specify a password. You may also see settings that let you hide the SSID, adjust the transmit power, and so on. Do not change these from their defaults unless you have a specific reason to do so.

After you have created a Wi-Fi network using your wireless hotspot feature, connect to it from your laptop or other device just as you would connect to your home network. If you have trouble connecting, reset your Galaxy S5 by holding the power button and tapping "Restart," and restart the other device as well before trying again.

By rooting your phone, you can enable Wi-Fi tethering without paying extra fees. Read more here (p. 264).

Preventing Extra Charges by Capping Your Data Usage

If you have a limited amount of bandwidth on your cell plan, you can set a hard limit to ensure your Galaxy S5 doesn't rack up overage charges. To set it, go to system settings → Data Usage and check "Set mobile data limit."

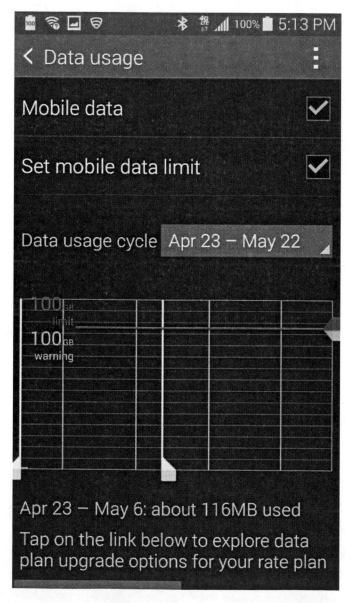

Set the data usage cycle appropriately, and then adjust the red slider up and down to specify the maximum amount of cellular data your Galaxy S5 is allowed to use during that period. As soon as you reach the limit, your Galaxy S5 will shut off cellular data. Of course, you can always return to this screen and uncheck "Set mobile data limit" if you need to.

Mirroring Your Galaxy S5's Screen on Another Display

The Galaxy S5's Screen Mirroring feature allows you to wirelessly share your Galaxy S5's screen on an external TV. Your Galaxy S5 can directly connect to newer Samsung wireless TVs with AllShare support, but if you don't have one—which most people don't—you must purchase a physical device from Samsung called the AllShare Cast Hub. At the time of publication, this device cost $99.99 from Samsung but was available at a substantial discount from third-party retailers such as Amazon.

Screen mirroring is useful for tasks such as streaming video or displaying photo galleries to an audience.

To use screen mirroring, go to system settings → Screen Mirroring. Ensure that the slider switch in the upper-right-hand corner of the screen is set to "On." You may need to put your TV or AllShare Cast Hub in sharing mode, so consult their instruction manuals if you are unsure. Once your Samsung TV or AllShare Cast Hub is prepared, your Galaxy S5 will automatically detect it. If it does not connect automatically, tap the device it detected and follow any required prompts.

> It's also possible to share your screen via a wired connection using a MHL 2.0 to HDMI adapter (street price $12.99).
>
> http://www.amazon.com/dp/B00ESM3Q7K/
>
> This option is cheaper but more cumbersome than a wireless solution. It may be suitable if you are on a budget and are mostly interested in streaming longer videos and movies during which you will not be holding or operating your Galaxy S5.

Disabling Annoying Sounds and Vibrations

By default, the Galaxy S5's interface makes a lot of blips and bloops. For those of us who relish peace and quiet, it is easy to disable them. Go to system settings → Sound. Uncheck some or all of the following:

- Dialing keypad tone

- Touch sounds

- Screen lock sound

- Haptic feedback

- Sound when tapped

- Vibrate when tapped

Personally, I also change my notification sound from "Whisper" to "Beep Once" (Tap Notifications → Media Storage → Just Once → "Beep Once"). "Beep Once" is more professional and less intrusive than the default notification sound.

Customizing the Notification Panel

You can customize the settings displayed in the notification panel by going to system settings → Notification Panel. Enable or disable the screen brightness adjustment setting found in the notification panel, and/or rearrange the toggle buttons. To rearrange buttons, simply tap, hold, and drag them. Releasing a toggle button over another toggle button on this screen will cause the two toggle buttons to swap places.

TalkBack Mode for Users Hard of Seeing

TalkBack is the main feature of the Galaxy S5 for users who have limited eyesight. Enable it in system settings → Accessibility → Vision → TalkBack.

When it is enabled, the entire TouchWiz experience changes. To use the device with TalkBack enabled, you drag your finger around the display, and the device selects different elements and speaks a description of them to you. For example, it will highlight buttons, menu items, and so on. Once you have successfully selected a screen element, you double-tap anywhere on the screen to activate it (the same as a single tap under normal circumstances). Scrolling is accomplished by swiping up and down with two fingers at once. Similarly, you pull down the notification panel by using two fingers, although you have to be very deliberate in this action. If you are having trouble, place your fingers close together and firmly swipe down from the top of the screen.

From system settings → Accessibility → Vision, you can also adjust the system font size, magnification gestures (discussed more, below), colors, and more.

Zooming In on Any Screen

The Galaxy S5 has a very cool zoom feature that allows you to triple tap on any screen to zoom in. Enable it in system settings → Accessibility → Vision → Magnification Gestures. Triple-tap anywhere to zoom in, and then pan using two fingers. You can also triple-tap and hold the third tap to temporarily zoom in.

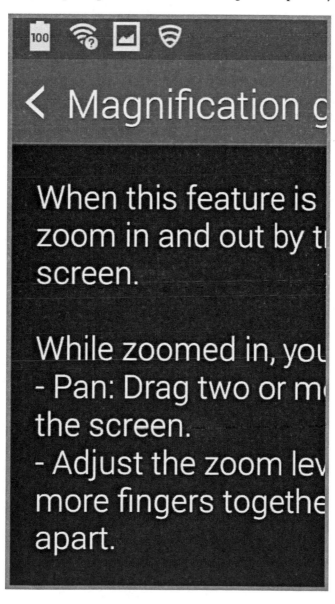

Blocking Unwanted Calls

The Galaxy S5 can block particular phone numbers, numbers containing certain values, and more. To block a contact in your Contacts app, open their details, tap the three-dot menu button, and then "Add to Reject List." When you receive a call from a number on your reject list, you won't know it at all.

To manage your reject list or to create a more sophisticated filter (e.g., block all 602 area codes), go to system settings → Call → Call Rejection.

Setting Up Auto Redial—Goodbye, Dropped Calls

The auto redial option makes dropped and failed calls a little less annoying. With this option enabled, your Galaxy S5 will automatically redial calls that fail to connect, or that drop in mid-conversation. To enable it, go to system settings → Call → Additional Settings and enable "Auto Redial."

Answering Calls Easily With the Home Button or Voice Commands

These are cool features that make it easier to answer phone calls that you do want. Go to system settings → Call → Answering and Ending Calls and enable "Pressing the Home key" and/or "Voice control."

In addition to swiping the green icon to answer incoming calls, you'll be able to simply hit the home button. Or, with voice control enabled, you can simply say "answer" or "reject" out loud.

Configuring Hands-Free Options and Voice Commands

The Galaxy S5 has some hands-free options that are useful if you drive a lot or otherwise have your hands full. Go to system settings → Language and Input → "Read notifications aloud" to have your Galaxy S5 speak callers' information, text messages, emails, and more out loud as notifications arrive.

Going Hands-Free With Car Mode

Car Mode gives you a simplified home screen, containing only options for placing calls, sending text messages, starting navigation, and playing music. It includes elements of the previous two tips. It looks like this:

Better yet, you can use all the features of Car Mode with your voice only.

To enable Car Mode, swipe down the notification panel with two fingers and tap "Car mode."

The first time you enter Car Mode, you will have to accept a legal disclaimer and configure S Voice if you have not already done so. Just follow the prompts and answer the questions you are asked. When you see a "Bluetooth permission request," tap "Yes." If your car stereo supports Bluetooth, follow the instructions to pair your Galaxy S5 with your car.

Once you have it configured and you see the main screen, just say "Hi Galaxy," wait for the tone, and then speak a command. For example:

- "Call John on mobile."

- "Play Daft Punk."

- "Navigate to Target."

When you receive an incoming call in Car Mode, say "Accept" or "Reject' out loud to answer or decline the call.

Configuring One-Handed Operation

Since the Galaxy S5 is a large device, Samsung has included some features to make one-handed use easier. Depending on the size of your hands and how you hold the Galaxy S5, you may or may not find these options useful.

Enable one-handed operation in system settings → One-Handed Operation. Once enabled, just swipe your thumb from the screen's edge to the middle and back to the edge to toggle one-handed mode. It looks like this:

Tap the upper-right-most icon (the rectangle with a diagonal arrow inside of it) to return to full-screen mode.

Seeing Helpful Information by Hovering Your Finger—Wait, What?

Air View is a very cool feature of the Galaxy S5—perhaps the coolest. It allows you to hover your finger above certain screen elements to see additional information. That's right—the Galaxy S5 can detect your finger even when you don't touch the screen. It does so using a technology from Synaptics called ClearPad®. Air View works in the Calendar, Gallery, Video, and Phone apps.

Turn on Air View in system settings → Air View. Here is an example of Air View in the Calendar app. I am hovering my finger above Saturday the 26th to preview events scheduled for that day.

☰ Month	Today	+ ⋮

<		April, 2014				>
Sun	Mon	Tue	Wed	Thu	Fri	Sat
30	31	1	2	3	4	5
6	7	8	9	10	11	12
13	14	15	16	17	18	19
20	21	Picnic				26
27	28	29	30	1	2	3
4	5	6	7	8	9	10

Configuring Motion Shortcuts

The Galaxy S5 supports some useful motion controls. For example, you can automatically call an on-screen contact by raising the Galaxy S5 to your ear, or silence it by placing it facedown on a surface. To enable these and other motions, go to system settings → Motions and Gestures.

Configuring Smart Screen Features

The Galaxy S5 has several experimental features that use the front camera to observe your face and perform actions accordingly. I think these features are curiosities more than anything else, but they are still interesting to try out, and may be a sign of things to come in future devices.

Smart Screen features include:

- **Smart Stay**: Keeps the screen on as long as you are looking at it, regardless of the screen timeout setting. Access it in system settings → Display.

- **Smart Rotation**: Rotates the screen according to the orientation of your face, overriding the default gravity sensor. Useful if you want to use the Galaxy S5 while lying on your side, as without Smart Rotation, the orientation will be wrong. Access it in system settings → Display → Screen Rotation.

- **Smart Pause**: Pause video when you look away from the screen. Works only in the Video and YouTube apps. Access it in system settings → Motions and Gestures → Mute/Pause.

- **Smart Scroll**: Detect your head movement to scroll web pages and lists automatically. Works only in Internet and Email apps. Access it in system settings → Accessibility → Dexterity and Interaction.

Enabling Glove Mode & Writing on the Screen With a Pencil

It is possible to increase the sensitivity of the Galaxy S5's screen in order to use it with gloves—and it works even with very thick ones. To do so, go to system settings → Display and enable "Increase touch sensitivity." If you leave this enabled when you don't need it, it's easier to have unintended screen taps, so make sure to turn it off when you're done.

This feature also allows you to tap and write on the screen with a regular pencil. I wouldn't recommend doing so unless you have a screen protector (p. 297) installed, but this feature is an interesting poor man's version of the Galaxy Note's S Pen feature.

Making Your Galaxy S5 Like New With a Factory Reset

Sometimes you need to wipe your Galaxy S5 completely—whether to sell it, or because it's gotten buggy and you want a fresh start. To factory reset your Galaxy S5, go to system settings → Backup and Reset → Factory data reset. Be warned that this will permanently erase everything on your internal storage. Make sure you've backed up all the files you need, or at least copied them to your SD card. And on that note, be aware that a factory reset will not affect an external SD card. If you wish to format your SD card, read on to the next tip.

Formatting Your SD Card

To format your SD card, go to system settings → Storage → Format SD Card. This will permanently wipe all the data on your external memory card, so be cautious. It's a good idea to do this when you get a new memory card to make sure that its file system is completely compatible with your Galaxy S5.

Never Miss a Notification With Smart Alert

How often do you pick up your Galaxy S5 throughout the day to check the LED light for notifications? I know I do it all the time. The Galaxy S5 has a special feature where it will vibrate upon being picked up if there are new notifications. This helps ensure you don't miss any notifications as you check throughout the day. To turn these on, go to system settings → Motions and Gestures → Smart Alert.

Using the Camera Flash for Notifications

The iPhone has offered flash notifications for a while, and Android is only starting to catch up. Fortunately, this option is available on the Galaxy S5—a powered-up version of the notification blinker that you can't miss... as long as your Galaxy S5 is face down! To enable this feature, go to system settings → Accessibility → Hearing and enable "Flash notification."

Hiding and Securing Files With Private Mode

Another new feature of the Galaxy S5 is Private Mode, which allows you to hide and secure files that you don't want anyone to accidentally see. It works in only a few select apps: Gallery, Video, Music, and Voice Recorder.

To use it, first swipe down the notification panel with two fingers to see the extended set of toggle buttons. Tap "Private mode."

Tap through the introductory screens and configure an unlock method for Private Mode (it can be different than the method you use to unlock your Galaxy S5). I suggest fingerprint mode or a PIN for a good balance of convenience and security.

Now, in the apps mentioned above, anytime you select a file and tap the three-dot menu icon, you will see the option "Move to private." When you move a file to private storage, it will be shown as long as Private Mode is enabled, but will completely disappear when Private Mode is disabled.

To view all the files in Private storage, open the app "My Files," swipe down, and tap "Private."

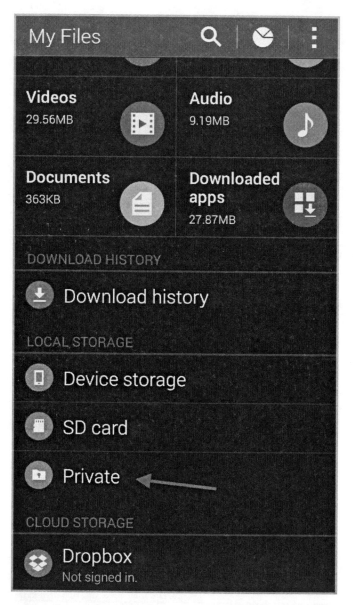

Remember—you have to turn off the Private Mode toggle button when you're done viewing your private content. If you forget to turn it off, your private files will be displayed along with all the others.

Tapping-to-Pay With Google Wallet

The Galaxy S5 contains an NFC (near-field communications) chip that uses RFID technology. This chip is compatible with tap-to-pay terminals found at establishments like 7-11, CVS, Walgreens, McDonalds, and more. With Google's free Wallet app, you can import your existing credit and debit cards and use your Galaxy S5 to tap and pay with them.

First, swipe the notification panel down with two fingers to see the <u>extended set of toggle buttons</u> (p. 56). Tap NFC to enable it.

Second, open the Google Play Store, search for "Google Wallet," and install the app.

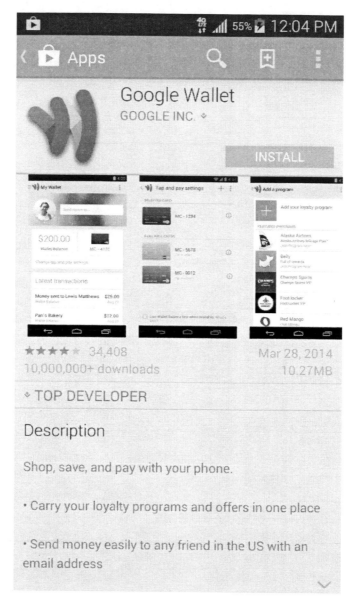

Open the app from your app drawer and sign in by tapping your email address and entering your ZIP code. You will have to create a PIN code for the Wallet app, so pick something you'll be sure to remember.

Once you are past setup, you may see this menu. If so, swipe from right to left to hide it.

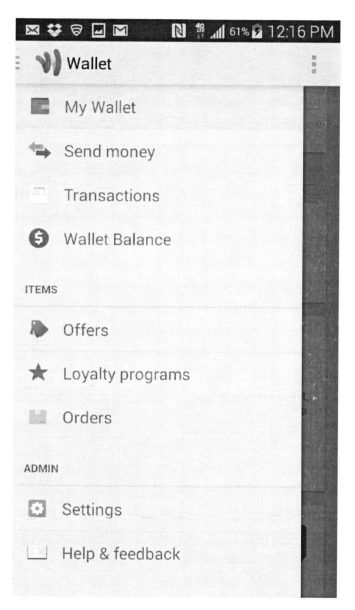

Then, tap "Set up tap and pay." Accept the terms of the agreement.

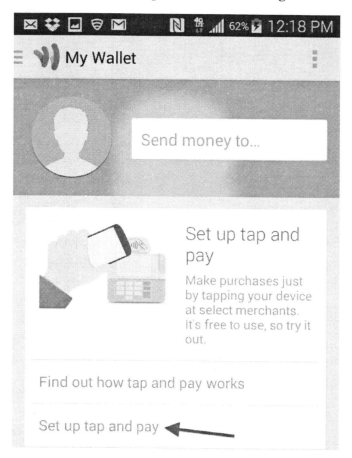

Tap "Next" and you will be asked to input your card details. Do so, or alternatively, tap "Scan your card" to import the details using your Galaxy S5's camera. (You have to line up the edges of the card exactly with the on-screen outline, or it will not work.)

After you have entered your details, tap "Add Card" at the bottom of the screen. You can then customize your card's name and appearance in the Google Wallet app. Then, tap "Next", and "Done" on the next screen.

Congrats! Now, as long as your NFC toggle is enabled, you can tap-to-pay at any compatible terminal. You don't need to open the Google Wallet app. Just touch the back of your Galaxy S5 to the terminal and enter your PIN code when prompted!

Now, if only tap-to-pay terminals would become more mainstream…

Managing Alarms and Timers

The Galaxy S5's Clock app is great for setting wake-up alarms or countdown timers. I frequently use the timer feature when I'm cooking; my only complaint is that you can't set more than one timer. (But you can by using Kitchen Timer, which I discuss in Chapter 9 (p. 280)!)

Alarms

This is the Clock app. To set an alarm for a specific time, select the "Alarm" tab and tap the plus (+) sign. Use the up and down arrows to set the hour and minute, and tap the AM/PM indicator to change it. Tap the days of the week to enable the alarm for them (you can have one alarm set for any day(s) of the week you want). Scroll down for snooze and other options.

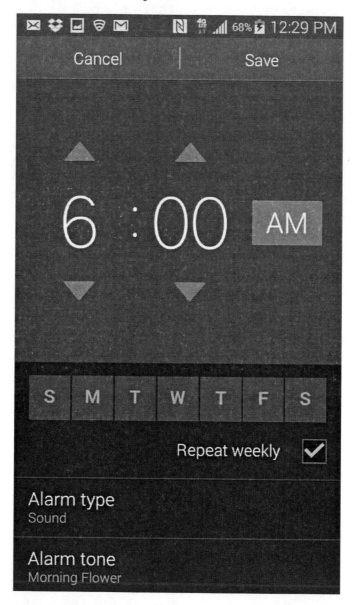

Timers

To set a timer, tap the "Timer" tab. Tap the numbers under "Hours," "Minutes," or "Seconds" to select the value you want to change, and then use the number pad to enter the desired value. Tap "Start" to start the timer.

Downloading Files Super Fast With Download Booster

The Galaxy S5 sports a new feature called Download Booster that combines your Wi-Fi and 4G LTE connections to download files super fast. However, in the United States, Sprint, AT&T, and Verizon have all blocked this feature. The only major U.S. carrier that has left it intact (at the time of writing) is T-Mobile. There are some indications that the other carriers will enable Download Booster at some point, but nothing is certain.

If you happen to have T-Mobile, here's how to use Download Booster. Swipe down the notification panel using two fingers to see the <u>extended toggle buttons</u> (p. 56). Enable "Download booster" by tapping it.

> On T-Mobile, you will have to disable Wi-Fi calling before Download booster will work. To do so, go to system settings → "More networks" and turn Wi-Fi calling off.

With Download Booster enabled, any time you start a high-bandwidth data activity, you will see this alert in your notification panel and you will notice your download speeds are amazing! Note that Download Booster only works with file downloads in the Internet browser, Chrome, YouTube, the Play Store, and a select few other apps. If you try to use it with a third-party app, it may or may not work.

Finally, if you have a limited data plan, keep an eye on your usage or consider <u>setting download limits</u> (p. 200) to avoid expensive overage charges. It's easy to go too crazy with Download Booster.

Using Quick Connect Mode to Easily Share Media With Nearby Devices

The Galaxy S line has slowly but steadily accumulated a vast selection of media sharing modes. If you had previous Galaxy S or Galaxy Note models, you probably remember things like Group Play, AllShare Cast, S Beam, Wi-Fi Direct, and other vaguely named media sharing apps.

Well, Samsung finally realized that these apps had gotten out of hand and none of their users understood what they were for or how to use them. So, it consolidated all of these features into Quick Connect Mode. This mode allows your Galaxy S5 to connect and share media with other nearby Galaxy devices, Samsung smart TVs, Galaxy Gear smart watches, and so on. No matter what kind of device you want to connect to, Quick Connect will guide you through the process and make it easy to share your photos, videos, or other files.

Access Quick Connect mode by swiping down the notification panel and tapping "Quick Connect."

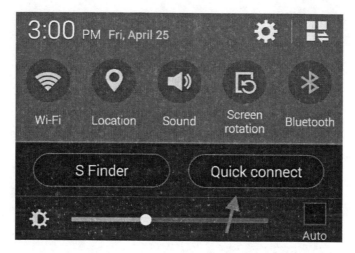

Searching Your Galaxy S5 Using S Finder

S Finder is a search engine that searches the data saved on your Galaxy S5. Let's say you want to find everything on your Galaxy S5 pertaining to your friend Mike Lee. Without S Finder, you would have to open each app individually to search for information—for example, searching for "Mike Lee" in the Phone app would turn up Mike's contact information, but not any text messages or e-mails in which he participated. S Finder solves this problem by providing a centralized search function for all apps. It can definitely come in handy, but it does have at least one major limitation: it doesn't support searching your Gmail inbox. Otherwise, it is quite effective.

Access S Finder by swiping down the notification panel and tapping "S Finder."

Taking Advantage of Free Gifts With Your Galaxy S5

Samsung has partnered with several third-party companies to offer free gifts and subscriptions with the Galaxy S5. These include:

- 3 months of free Bitcasa 1TB secure cloud storage ($30 value)

- $5 Blurb coupon toward creating a printed photo book

- $15 in-game credits for Cut the Rope 2

- 6 month subscription to EasilyDo Pro, a time management app

- Flick Dat contact manager app ($1.99 value)

- 3 months of LinkedIn Premium ($75 value)

- 6 months free Skimble premium service, a workout coach app

- 12 month subscription to Bloomberg BusinessWeek+ app

- 6 months of 50GB Box.net storage ($18 value)

- 2 years of 50GB Dropbox storage ($100 value)

- 3 months of Evernote's Premium service ($15 value)

- 1 year of Lark premium service, a personal wellness assistant app ($36 value)

- 6 months of MapMyRun/MapMyRide premium service ($35.94 value)

- 1 year of free RunKeeper service, a personal fitness trainer app ($19.99 value)

- 6 month subscription to The Wall Street Journal ($138 value)

To take advantage of these free promotions, find the adjacent home screen with the Galaxy Gifts widget, and tap it. Download any apps that you want, and upon installing them, you will receive your free gifts or instructions on how to redeem them. If you previously removed this widget, see instructions on <u>adding widgets</u> (p. 52) to re-add it to one of your home screens.

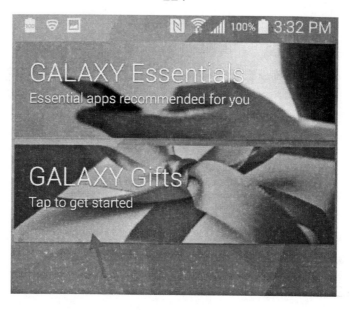

In my opinion, the best of the gifts is the Dropbox storage. However, if your Dropbox account currently has a Samsung promotion applied to it (from a previous Galaxy phone promotion), you will <u>not</u> receive the space unless you wait to log in to Dropbox on your Galaxy S5 until the previous promotion expires. This is extremely disappointing—to say the least—but there's nothing you can do about it unless you're willing to forgo logging into Dropbox until your old promotion expires.

Getting a Floating App Tray—The Toolbox

The Toolbox is a new feature on the Galaxy S5. It's like a floating app tray—it appears as a small white circle on all screens. When you tap it, it expands to show app shortcuts. You can customize it to show whatever app shortcuts you would like.

Enable the Toolbox by swiping down the notification panel with two fingers, and enabling "Toolbox."

To customize the app shortcuts available in the Toolbox, tap, hold, and drag it to the "Edit" button at the top of the screen. Release it.

Authenticating PayPal Payments Using Your Fingerprint

In addition to securing your lock screen (p. 187) and Private Mode (p. 211), the fingerprint scanner can also be used to authenticate PayPal payments. To set this up, first go to system settings → Finger Scanner → Pay with PayPal. Tap "Install" to install FIDO Ready, a necessary software library.

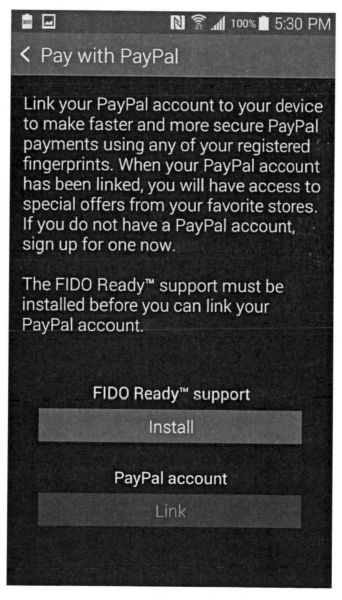

Then, you will be able to tap the "Link" button to connect the fingerprint scanner to your PayPal account. Follow the instructions and log into your PayPal account. If you have not already enrolled a fingerprint on your Galaxy S5, you will be required to do so. If you do, tap the back button when you're finished to return to

PayPal. You will be required to swipe your finger one more time to verify your fingerprint with PayPal. Then, install the PayPal app from the Google Play Store. Any time you make a PayPal payment on your Galaxy S5, you will be able to swipe your finger instead of entering your password!

Downloading and Applying App and OS Updates

Fortunately, Android makes it very easy to update your apps and operating system. For apps that you've downloaded from the Google Play Store, you will receive automatic update notifications in your notification panel. Often, updates will install themselves and you will only need to clear the notification. On occasion, you will need to manually approve an update, in which case you simply need to tap on the notification and follow the prompts. You can also check for updates by opening the Google Play Store, swiping from the left edge of the screen to the right to bring up the menu, and tapping "My Apps."

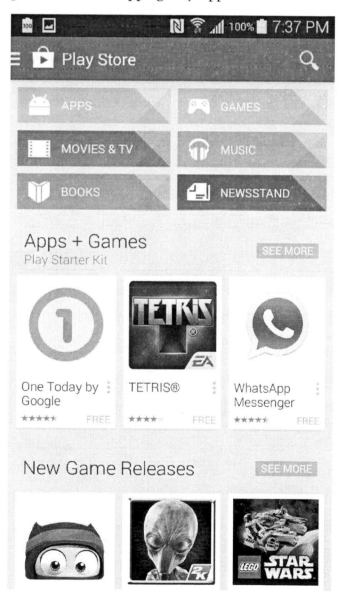

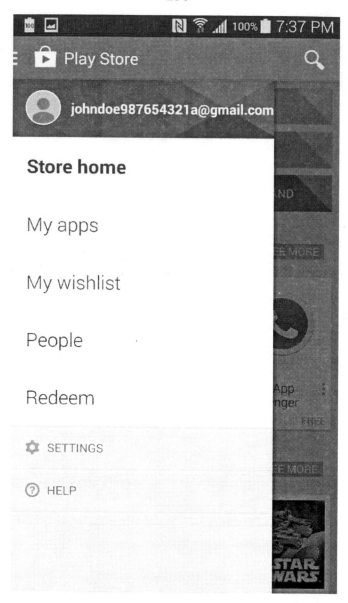

If you have apps with available updates, you will see them on this screen.

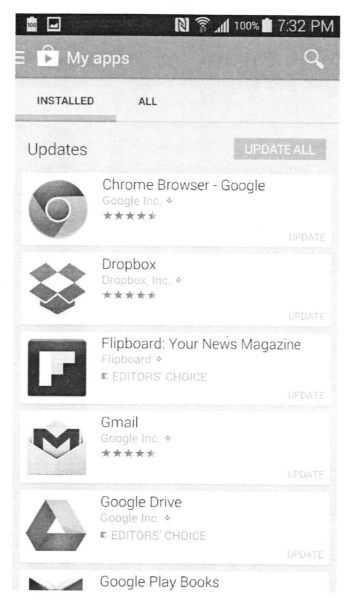

Similarly, you will receive a notification if there is an operating system or carrier update available. To install the update, just tap the notification in the notification panel and follow the prompts provided. Alternatively, you can manually check for updates by going to system settings → "About device" and tap "Software update."

Keeping Your Galaxy S5 Awake While Charging

The longest available screen timeout setting on the Galaxy S5 is 10 minutes. Sometimes this isn't enough. For example, when I use AirDroid (p. 281), an app that (among other things) lets me use my desktop web browser to send and receive texts on my Galaxy S5, I don't want my phone to go to sleep at all.

Fortunately, there's a way to accomplish this. Go to system settings → "About device." Swipe down until you see "Build number." Now, start repeatedly tapping this box. You will see a message that you are about to become a developer. Keep going until Developer Mode is activated.

Now, hit the back button. You will see a new option in system settings called "Developer options." Tap this, and then check "Stay awake." Done! As long as your Galaxy S5 is plugged in and charging, it will not go to sleep.

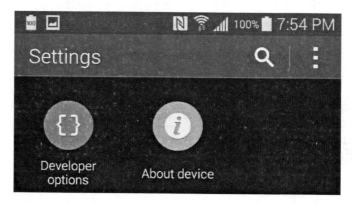

Taking Screenshots

Want to take screenshots on your Galaxy S5 like the ones included in this book? Just press and hold the home and power buttons together for approximately one second, until the screen flashes. Your screenshot will be saved in your Gallery with the rest of your photos.

Maintaining Peace of Mind With Blocking Mode (Do Not Disturb)

The Galaxy S5's Do Not Disturb mode is called "Blocking Mode." It allows you to set quiet hours during which your Galaxy S5 will not display or sound notifications.

Access it by going to system settings → "Blocking mode." Turn it on by tapping the on-off button in the upper-right-hand corner of the screen.

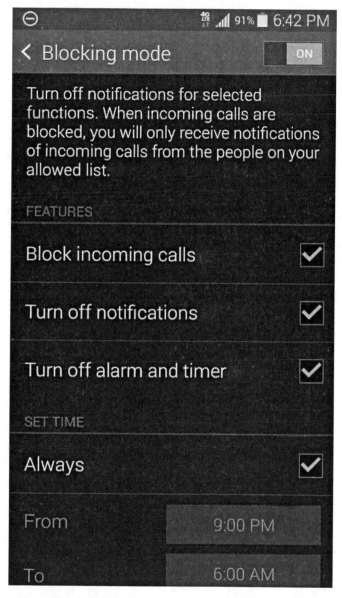

Then, select the types of notifications you want to block. You can block calls only, notifications only, alarms and timers, or any combination of those things. You can also swipe down and tap "Allowed contacts" to set exceptions (for example, your kids). To select one contact at a time from your Contacts app, choose the "Custom" option.

Note that if you have "Always" checked, Blocking Mode will stay on until you turn it off. To automatically schedule blocking mode for a certain time of day or night, uncheck "Always" and set a custom time. Unfortunately, you cannot configure blocking mode to kick in during multiple, non-continuous periods of the day.

Conserving Battery Power With the S5's Power Saving Modes

The Galaxy S5 has two power saving modes: regular Power Saving Mode and Ultra Power Saving Mode. Regular Power Saving Mode works by dimming the screen and restricting CPU performance. Turn it on by swiping down the notification panel with two fingers and tapping "Power saving."

You can also tap and hold "Power saving" to access advanced options. Specifically, you can configure power saving mode to block all data transfer by background apps, use grayscale mode (black-and-white), and more. I would suggest enabling grayscale mode before blocking background data, because the latter can seriously interfere with your apps, possibly leading to missed notifications or alarms.

On the other hand, Ultra Power Saving Mode takes things even further. In addition to forcing grayscale mode, dimming the backlight, and restricting CPU performance, it deactivates Wi-Fi and Bluetooth, deactivates the 4G cellular radio when the screen is off, and limits you to a few select apps. You will only want to use Ultra Power Saving Mode if you absolutely need to conserve your battery power down to the last drop. It is similar to the power conservation features of <u>Emergency Mode</u> (p. 35) but without the safety features.

Turn it on by swiping down the notification panel with two fingers and tapping "U. power saving."

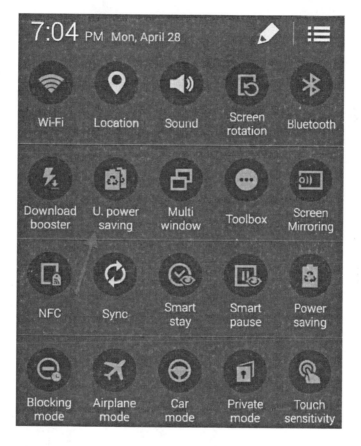

Accessing Kids Mode

The Galaxy S5's Kids Mode allows you to set up a "sandbox" environment for young kids. It contains various fun apps and games that entertain your kids without allowing them to screw up your phone.

Kids Mode must be downloaded before you can use it. To do so, go to the home screen and <u>add a widget</u> (p. 52). Find the Kids Mode 1x1 widget and add it to your home screen. Then, tap it and follow the prompts to download and install the app.

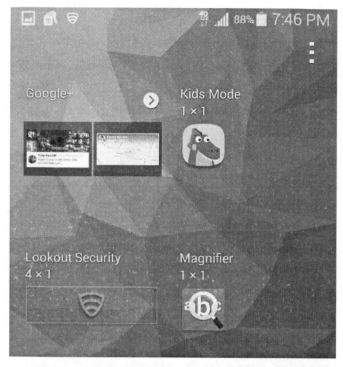

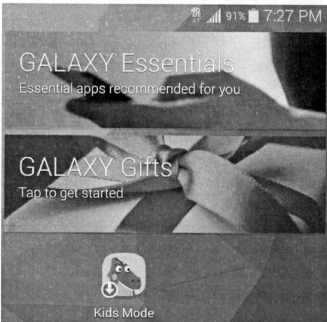

After you have done so, the 1x1 widget will be replaced by the Kids Mode app, and an icon will also appear in your app drawer. Tap it to launch Kids Mode.

When you first launch Kids Mode, you will need to set a PIN used for disabling Kids Mode in the future and enter your child's name and date of birth. You will also be prompted to select which, if any, third-party apps will be allowed in Kids Mode.

To change parental controls (e.g., a time limit, etc.) or exit Kids Mode, tap the icons in the bottom-right-hand corner of the screen, as shown in the above screenshot. If you forget your PIN code while Kids Mode is engaged, you will need to remove the battery from your Galaxy S5 to reboot it.

Using Your Galaxy S5 as a Magnifying Glass

The Galaxy S5 comes with a widget that allows you to use the camera and flash LED as an illuminated magnifying lens, and the feature works quite well. To use it, go to the home screen and add a widget (p. 52). Swipe until you see the Magnifier widget, and add it.

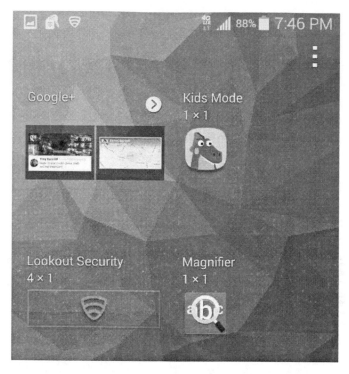

Then, tap the Magnifier widget on your home screen to launch it.

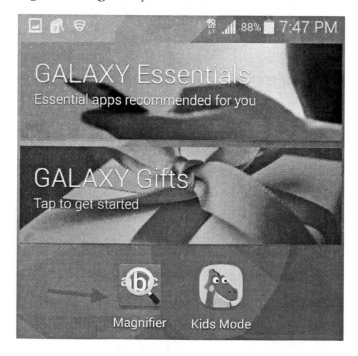

Tap anywhere on the screen or tap the "Focus" button to autofocus the image. If the camera refuses to focus, move your Galaxy S5 away from the object you are trying to focus on. Adjust the zoom level with the slider on the bottom of the screen, and turn on illumination and/or capture a photograph using the other buttons at the top of the screen.

S Health: Managing Your Diet, Exercise, and Fitness

Samsung has heavily marketed the health and fitness features of the Galaxy S5, and all of these features are accessible through the S Health app. S Health can help you manage all aspects of your exercise and diet.

The first time you open S Health form your app drawer, you will follow a series of prompts asking you to consent to the terms of use, sign into a Samsung account to compare your stats with other users, and enter your personal information and measurements.

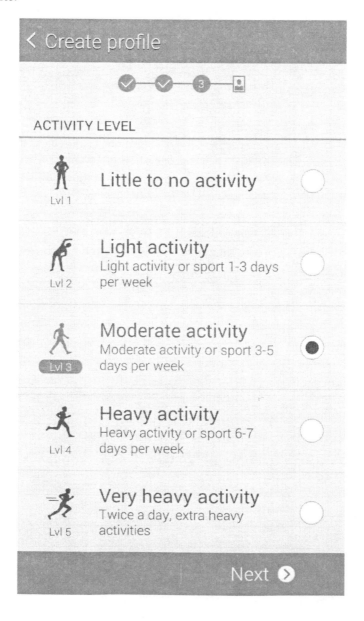

During this process, you may be asked to update S Health and/or HealthService. If so, proceed with the update.

In S Health, tap the upper-left-hand corner of the screen to bring up the main menu:

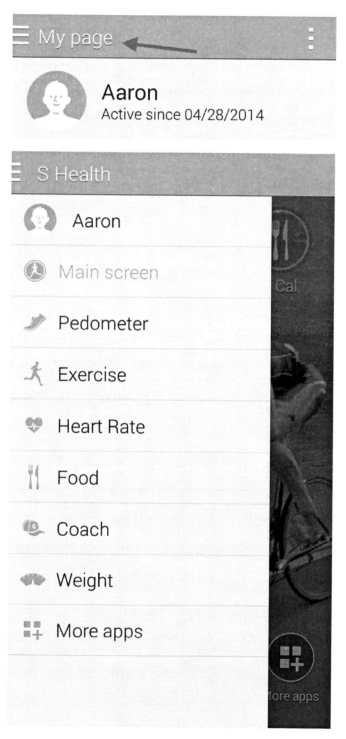

- **(Your name):** View a summary of the day's activity, calories burned, and calories consumed.

- **Main screen:** View a "home screen" with quick shortcuts to the pedometer, exercise log, and heart rate monitor.

- **Pedometer:** Start and stop the pedometer, which counts steps taken. The pedometer runs in the background, even when you aren't using S Health, as long as it has been started. You may want to disable the pedometer if you're riding a bumpy train or doing something that could register as false steps, but otherwise you can simply start the pedometer and leave it that way for as long as you like (weeks, months, etc.).

- **Exercise:** Set a workout goal and record your activity. Use this screen right before you work out. Tap the type of exercise you plan to do (running, walking, cycling, or hiking), then tap "Set workout goal" and enter information, and then tap "Start." S Health will monitor your workout and record your information.

- **Heart Rate:** Use the built-in heart rate monitor to take a measurement. You can use this throughout your workout, or any time you like and S Health will catalog the data. To use the heart rate monitor, place the tip of your index finger over the camera flash on the back of the Galaxy S5, pointing up .Do not press too hard or the reading may fail.

- **Food:** Record what you eat for each meal of the day and count your calories.

- **Coach:** This feature collects information about you and your lifestyle and suggests fitness goals to program into S Health on the (Your name) screen.

- **Weight:** Record your weight. The more often, the better (for example, once per day).

On all of these screens, there is a green triangle in the lower-right-hand corner of the screen. Tap it to view historical information that S Health has collected.

Overall, the key to using S Health is to be diligent in inputting your information, keep the pedometer enabled, and use its features as much as possible. The more data is gathers about you, the better it can help you manage your goals.

If you have a companion device that is compatible with S Health, you can configure it to wirelessly sync with your Galaxy S5 to help automate the process of inputting data. To view a list of compatible devices, tap the three-dot menu icon in S Health and then "Compatible accessories."

Purchasing Movies, Books, Magazines and Other Media From Google Play

The Galaxy S5 comes preloaded with five "store" apps: Play Books, Play Games, Play Movies & TV, Play Music, and Play Newsstand.

These are the easiest and most seamless way to purchase entertainment media for your Galaxy S5. Want to watch some Breaking Bad? Open Play Movies & TV and purchase episodes for $1.99 each—they'll be yours to view for life. Want to read *1984*? Open Play Books and buy it for $5.74.

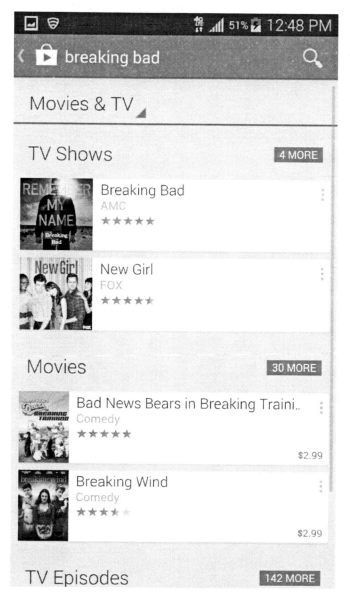

All of these apps let you 1) purchase media and 2) view that media. They're all-in-one packages.

Of course, if you already have large media collections on other platforms (e.g., Amazon Kindle or iTunes), you may want to download those apps from the Google Play Store to keep your media collections consolidated with one company. But if you're not already invested in other platforms, Google is a good place to start.

Viewing and Editing Microsoft Office Documents

The Galaxy S5 comes preloaded with POLARIS Office, a Microsoft Word, Excel, and PowerPoint viewer and editor. Let me level with you, though—Microsoft Office editing on Android really isn't ready for prime time. Although you can create or edit documents, only basic features are supported and compatibility isn't 100%. If you have a document that needs precise formatting, you can't use POLARIS because you'll more than likely end up with corrupted formatting when you open the file on your computer. Besides, it's not possible to do serious work on a 5.1" screen.

However, for just viewing Office documents, POLARIS is quite good. It doesn't always render things exactly like you'd see on your computer, but it almost always does a good enough job to get you the information you need.

Creating or Opening Documents

From the POLARIS main screen, you can tap a recent document's thumbnail image to open it, or tap the plus (+) sign in the upper-right-hand corner of the screen to create a new document. Or, use the File Browser in the lower-left-hand corner of the screen to find and open a file saved on your Galaxy S5's internal memory or SD card.

You can also open files you receive as email attachments. Let's use Gmail as an example, although the process will be very similar in other email apps.

Here, I have sent myself an email with a .DOCX attachment.

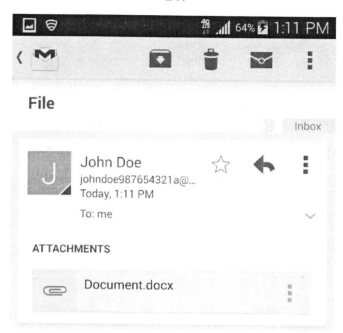

Upon simply tapping it once, the file is opened in POLARIS.

Managing Documents

There are a lot of features to explore in POLARIS, but the most important actions on the editing screen are as follows:

- Tap the filename in the upper-left-hand corner to save the document, save it as a new file, export it to a PDF file, sent it as an email attachment, or <u>print</u> (p. 249) it.

- Tap the plus sign in the upper-right hand corner to insert new elements like images and tables.

- Tap and hold text or other elements to select them and then tap the wrench icon in the upper-right-hand corner to modify the elements' properties. For example, if you select text and then tap this button, you can change the font, font size, color, and so on.

- Tap the three horizontal lines in the upper-right-hand corner to access settings including view-only mode, which simplifies the interface and prevents you from accidentally modifying your document.

- Tap once anywhere in the document to position the cursor and open the keyboard to start typing.

> As I mentioned above, POLARIS shines for viewing Office documents—not editing them. If you really, really need to edit Microsoft Office documents on your Galaxy S5 without corrupting their formatting, try downloading Microsoft Office Mobile from the Google Play Store. It's completely free to download and use, and won't destroy a document's formatting. However, it is more limited in the types of edits it can make.

Printing With Google Cloud Print

Google Cloud Print is relatively new software from Google that makes it easy to print documents from your Galaxy S5.

First, you will need to set up your printer with Google Cloud Print. On your desktop or laptop computer, go to the link below. If your printer connects to your computer via USB, click the "Add Classic Printer" button and follow the instructions. If your printer has Wi-Fi or is connected to the Internet via an Ethernet cable, click the "Add Cloud Ready Printer" button instead. After you have configured your printer in this way, you will be able to print to it over the Internet at any time using your Galaxy S5.

> **http://www.google.com/landing/cloudprint/**

Once your printer is configured, open the Google Play Store on your Galaxy S5 and search for "Cloud Print." Download and install the app.

Once installed, you will receive a notification in your notification panel. Tap it to enable the Cloud Print service. If you don't see the notification, instead go to system settings → Printing → Cloud Print and change the slider from "off" to "on." If you have already set up your printer using your computer, you will see its name on this screen. This means you are ready to print.

Now, in any app that has a print function (like POLARIS Office), you will be able to wirelessly print using your printer via Cloud Print!

Chapter 7: Advanced Functions

By now, we've discussed nearly everything there is to discuss about the Galaxy S5, at least as it comes in the box. In this chapter, you'll learn how to extend the functionality of your Galaxy S5 and become a power user yourself.

Connecting To Your PC

Installing USB Drivers

Some Android devices support USB Mass Storage Mode out of the box, meaning that computers will automatically mount them as flash drives when connected over USB. Unfortunately, the Galaxy S5 is not one of these devices. If you connect your Galaxy S5 to your PC via USB without first installing the proper drivers, you will only see a lot of failure dialogs.

To remedy this situation on Windows, you need to download Samsung's drivers. Click "See all downloads" and then the EXE icon to download and install the package on your computer. Don't worry if you have a carrier other than Sprint—the USB drivers are the same.

http://www.samsung.com/us/support/owners/product/ SM-G900PZKASPR

(Short URL: http://goo.gl/hWYURk)

On Mac OS, you don't need any Samsung-specific drivers, but you do need the official Android File Transfer tool

http://www.android.com/filetransfer/

Accessing Files

On Windows, once you have properly installed the Samsung USB drivers, you can open your Galaxy S5 as you would a flash drive. If AutoPlay opens, click "Open device to view files."

If AutoPlay does not open, open Windows Explorer and go to Computer →
(Name of your Galaxy S5).

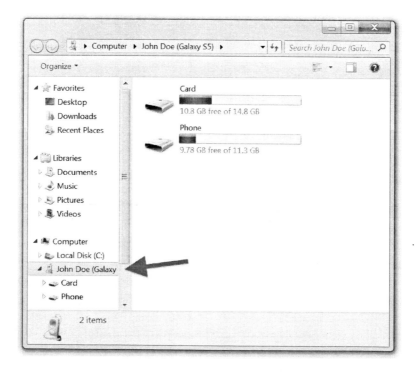

Once you have accessed your Galaxy S5, you can open "Phone" to view its
internal storage or "Card" to view the contents of its external SD card. You can
copy, paste, and move files just as you would anywhere else on your PC.

Be very careful about deleting or moving system or app files—only do so if you have a specific reason to and you know what you're doing.

On Mac OS, Android File Transfer will open as soon as you plug in your Galaxy S5's USB cable. Click "Phone" and "Card" to view internal and SD storage, respectively. You can drag files in and out of this window as if it were a Finder window.

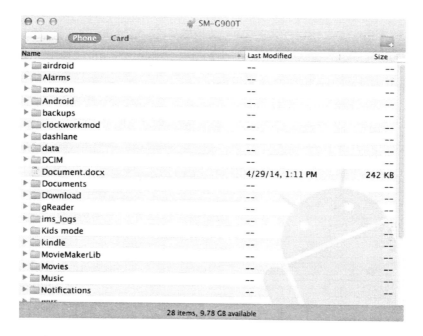

If your Galaxy S5 is having trouble connecting to your computer via USB, make sure USB debugging is switched off in system settings → Developer Options (p. 231).

Backing Up Your Data With Samsung Kies

In addition to managing your Galaxy S5's file system, you can also take advantage of the backup and media management tools built into Samsung Kies, Samsung's synchronization software. It is available for both Windows and Mac OS. I cover only the Windows version below, because the Mac OS version is identical.

Download the appropriate version of Kies from this link (version 3.0 or greater), and install it on your desktop or laptop computer.

http://www.samsung.com/us/kies/

Kies is pretty straightforward and intuitive. It does two things: backup/restore of various types of data on your Galaxy S5, and management of your photos, music, video, etc.

It's a good idea to regularly backup your Galaxy S5 with Kies, although it's generally not necessary to backup every single type of data you can. For example, all of your Contacts should be consolidated in your Google account, so there should be no need to back them up with Kies. However, the ability to backup other data like apps and text messages can be very useful.

> If you plan to root your Galaxy S5, you can perform Nandroid backups instead of Kies backups. Nandroid backups can be saved to your SD card and create an *exact* image of your device. To do so, use the backup and restore controls available in your custom recovery.

Remote Controlling Your Galaxy S5 With AirDroid

AirDroid is a free third-party app that allows you to control your Galaxy S5 using the web browser on your desktop or laptop computer. You can transfer files, view photos, edit contacts, and more. My personal favorite is the SMS function—it allows you to send and receive text messages on your computer. If you're having a long text conversation, it's much easier to type on a real keyboard than on your Galaxy S5's screen.

Get AirDroid from the Play Store on your Galaxy S5. Install it, and make sure your Galaxy S5 is connected to the same Wi-Fi network as your PC. Start AirDroid, and your Galaxy S5 will guide you through the setup process. You can create an account with AirDroid if you wish, which will give you access to additional features such as Find Phone, but it is not necessary. Also, it is possible to pair your Galaxy S5 with your PC by scanning a QR code instead of entering a PIN, which is a nice feature.

I suggest you experiment with AirDroid to see how it's most useful for you. As I mentioned, its number one feature for me is text message control.

Rooting Your Galaxy S5 to Unlock More Power

If you've spent any time on Android discussion forums, you've probably seen people talking about "rooting" their phones. What does this mean, and why would you want to do it?

As you may know, Android is based on Linux, and in Linux (and all Unix-based systems) the most privileged administrator account is called the "root" account. With root privileges, it is possible to execute any code you wish—code that is not normally possible to run.

Here are some things you can do after rooting your Galaxy S5:

- Block all advertisements in browsers and apps

- Share your cellular connection over Wi-Fi even if you don't pay for your carrier's hot spot option

- Backup your apps with Titanium Backup

- Install custom ROMs, versions of the Android OS that enthusiasts have modified, de-bloated, or otherwise improved

- Permanently delete bloatware

- Use Greenify to freeze background apps and save battery power

- … and much more.

In this section, I will show you how to do all of these things.

KNOX Warning

Before we get to the good stuff, I want to give you a word of warning. The Galaxy S5 has a built-in security layer called Samsung KNOX, a group of features that's targeted toward commercial and enterprise companies. To make a long story short, KNOX helps Samsung sell Galaxy S5s to corporate customers who want to protect their data. It's not anything the average user will use—or even be aware of—but it's relevant if you're planning to root your device. Here's why.

The Galaxy S5 has something called a KNOX security flag, which is permanently tripped when you root it. After the KNOX security flag is tripped, the Galaxy S5 will no longer run the KNOX environment and, importantly, its warranty is voided. If you void your Galaxy S5's warranty in this way, Samsung has the right to withhold support from you in the future.

That said, thousands of users have chosen to root their Samsung devices and void the KNOX warranty. As long as your Galaxy S5 never needs service from Samsung, it won't matter. Ultimately, you have to decide whether the pros outweigh the cons. Personally, I think they do, and I have chosen to root my Galaxy S5 and void my warranty. (However, I also have an insurance plan through my carrier, and they don't care about the KNOX status of the phone. If you want to root your Galaxy S5 but still have some form of hardware support, I suggest you do some Googling and learn your carrier's policy on KNOX.)

If you still want to root your Galaxy S5 and/or install a custom ROM, continue reading.

Carrier Warnings

At the time of publication, not all carriers' Galaxy S5s can be rooted. As of May 2014, this is the status of each major Galaxy S5 variant:

Sprint	**Yes**
T-Mobile	**Yes**
AT&T	No
Verizon	No
US Cellular	**Yes**

If you have an international device or a carrier not listed here, check the following link to see whether rooting is supported for your model. Also, if you have AT&T

or Verizon, remember that by the time you're reading this book, it may be possible to root your device. You should also check the following link.

http://forum.xda-developers.com/showpost.php?p=51421228

(Short URL: http://goo.gl/QUQci9)

Overview

WARNING: This procedure will void your warranty and permanently trip your KNOX flag. Furthermore, you must have a Sprint, T-Mobile, or US Cellular Galaxy S5. AT&T and Verizon users cannot root or install custom ROMs at the time of publication.

If you want to root and/or install a custom ROM, there are really three separate steps:

1. **Root**

2. **Install a custom recovery (used to install a custom ROM; optional)**

3. **Install a custom ROM (optional)**

To root, you will use software called CF-Auto-Root, and you will need access to a Windows computer and SD card. It is not possible to complete this process with a Mac OSX computer (even virtual machines like VMWare and Parallels will not work).

Let's get started.

Rooting

First, go to system settings → About Device and write down your model number. It will be something like SM-G900T. Then, follow these instructions precisely:

1. **Ensure you have backed up your critical data**. Use <u>Kies</u> (p. 253) if necessary.

2. Install the <u>Samsung USB drivers</u> (p. 251) on your computer.

3. Download the latest version of ODIN here (get v3.09 or newer) and install it on your computer.

> **<u>http://forum.xda-developers.com/showthread.php?t=2189539</u>**
>
> **(Short URL: <u>http://goo.gl/ednI59</u>)**

4. Go to the following page and download the appropriate ZIP file for your Galaxy S5's model number.

> **<u>http://forum.xda-developers.com/showpost.php?p=51421228</u>**
>
> **(Short URL: <u>http://goo.gl/QUQci9</u>)**

5. Extract the .zip file, but do not extract the resulting .tar.md5 file.

6. Make sure your Galaxy S5 is unplugged from your computer and completely powered down (hold the power key and tap "Power off").

7. Hold Volume Down + Home + Power on your Galaxy S5 until it boots into download mode. It may ask you to press Volume Up to continue; do so.

8. Start ODIN on your computer (Odin3-vX.X.exe).

9. Click the "PDA" button in ODIN and load the .tar.md5 file you extracted earlier.

10. Connect your Galaxy S5 and computer via USB. Do not use a USB hub.

11. Uncheck the "Repartition" checkbox if it is checked in ODIN.

12. Click "Start" and wait for your Galaxy S5 to reboot. Do NOT touch your Galaxy S5 until it has fully rebooted.

That's it—your Galaxy S5 is rooted. If you have trouble, seek help in this thread.

> **http://forum.xda-developers.com/showthread.php?p=51421228**
>
> **(Short URL: http://goo.gl/nc0jLs)**

Installing a Custom Recovery

Now, you need to install a custom recovery, if you want to install a custom ROM or perform Nandroid backups (p. 254).

1. Go to the following link and download the most recently posted .tar.md5 file.

> **http://goo.im/devs/philz_touch/CWM_Advanced_Editi on/klte**
>
> **(Short URL: http://goo.gl/OveSdC)**

2. Make sure your Galaxy S5 is unplugged from your computer and completely powered down (hold the power key and tap "Power off").

3. Hold Volume Down + Home + Power on your Galaxy S5 until it boots into download mode. It may ask you to press Volume Up to continue; do so.

4. Start ODIN on your computer (Odin3-vX.X.exe).

5. Click the "PDA" button in ODIN and load the .tar.md5 file you just downloaded.

6. Connect your Galaxy S5 and computer via USB. Do not use a USB hub.

7. Uncheck the "Repartition" checkbox if it is checked in ODIN.

8. Click "Start" and wait for your Galaxy S5 to reboot. Do NOT touch your Galaxy S5 until it has fully rebooted.

Now, you've successfully installed your custom recovery.

Installing a Custom ROM

To find and download a custom ROM, go to the XDA Sprint Galaxy S5 development forum or the T-Mobile Galaxy S5 development forum. Browse through the various threads tagged [ROM] until you find something that appeals to you.

> **http://forum.xda-developers.com/sprint-galaxy-s5/development**
>
> **http://forum.xda-developers.com/tmobile-galaxy-s5/development**

> You may see odexed and deodexed versions of custom ROMs. I suggest always using the deodexed version; the odexed version can be faster at initial boot, but deodexed ROMs are nearly as fast, and more importantly, are required for many flashable themes and other mods.

If the custom ROM you select has installation instructions, follow them. Otherwise, follow this procedure:

1. **Ensure you have backed up your critical data**. Use Kies if necessary.

2. Download the custom ROM .zip file. Do NOT unzip it.

3. Transfer the .zip file to your Galaxy S5's external SD card.

4. Power your Galaxy S5 off completely, and restart it in recovery mode (hold Volume Up + Home + Power).

5. Tap "Backup and Restore," and then "Backup to /storage/sdcard1." This will create a full backup of your device and save it onto your external SD card in case something goes wrong with the installation process.

6. When the backup is finished, return to the main menu and tap "Wipe Data/Factory Reset." Tap "Wipe Data/Factory Reset," wait for it to complete, and then tap "Clean to Install a New ROM" and wait for it to complete.

7. Return to the main menu and tap "Install ZIP," and then "Choose zip from /storage/sdcard1."

8. Locate the .zip file on your SD card and follow the prompts to install it.

9. After installation has finished, return to the main menu and tap "Reboot System Now." If it prompts you with "Rom may flash stock recovery..." tap "No."

That's it! Your Galaxy S5 will restart into your new ROM. Enjoy, and feel free to repeat the process to try out other custom ROMs.

Things to Do After You've Rooted Your Galaxy S5

Installing BusyBox

After rooting your Galaxy S5 with CF-Auto-Root, your first order of business is installing BusyBox, which is a prerequisite to many other root apps.

Open the Google Play Store on your Galaxy S5 and search for "BusyBox." Find the BusyBox app published by Stephen (Stericson) and install it. Open the app, tap "Install," and wait until you see the message, "It looks like the installation of BusyBox was successful." Then, reboot your Galaxy S5.

> Now that you're rooted, you may see "Superuser" requests when you attempt to use root apps. You need to grant these requests, or the root-enabled features of your apps will not work.

Blocking Ads With AdAway

One of the best things you can do after you've rooted is to block ads. There are several apps designed for this purpose, but I have found AdAway to be the best. It blocks advertisements everywhere on your device—in the stock browser, in Chrome, and in apps.

AdAway is not on the Google Play Store; it is on an alternative platform called F-Droid. Download F-Droid at the link below and install it to your Galaxy S5. Search for "AdAway" in F-Droid and install it by tapping the latest version number at the bottom of the screen. Open AdAway, tap the button entitled "Download files and apply ad blocking." Reboot your Galaxy S5 when the process is done, and your Galaxy S5 will be ad-free!

https://f-droid.org/

Backing Up With Titanium Backup

Titanium Backup is an app that allows you to backup and restore your other apps to an SD card. It's most useful when you are installing a new custom ROM—it's much easier to backup and restore your apps using Titanium Backup than to re-download everything from the Play Store. Plus, it backs up your app settings.

The free version of Titanium Backup performs basic backups and restores but purchasing a pro key gives you many more options (~$5.99 on the Google Play Store).

Before using Titanium Backup for the first time, you will need to enable USB debugging. To do so, go to system settings → About Device. Double-tap on "Build number" repeatedly and you will get a notification that developer options have been enabled. Go back to General settings, tap "Developer options," switch the slider in the upper-right-hand corner of the screen to "On," and tick the checkbox next to "USB debugging."

> In some cases, enabling USB debugging can prevent a proper USB connection with your computer. If you are having trouble connecting over USB after enabling USB debugging, try disabling it again.

To perform a backup with Titanium Backup, open the app and tap the checkmark in the upper-right-hand corner of the screen.

Next, tap the "Run" button next to "Backup all user apps."

Deselect any apps you do not want to backup, and then tap the green checkmark in the upper-right-hand corner of the screen. Your Galaxy S5 will back up all of your apps, app data, and system data your internal storage (/storage/emulated/legacy/TitaniumBackup. Use ES File Explorer to copy the backup folder to your external SD card. (The current version of Titanium Backup has a bug that will not allow it to directly write to the SD card, which is why you must use ES File Explorer.)

To restore a backup, first use ES File Explorer to copy the TitaniumBackup folder from your SD card to /storage/emulated/legacy on your internal storage. Then, open Titanium Backup, tap the checkmark, and tap "Restore missing apps with data."

WARNING: It is okay to restore apps and app data when moving to a new custom ROM, but never restore system data on a new custom ROM, or you will cause a multitude of errors and have to start over from scratch.

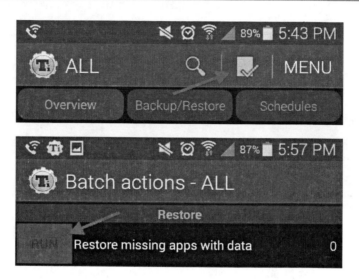

From the next screen, select all of the apps you wish to restore and tap the green checkmark in the upper-right-hand corner of the screen.

That's all there is to it—unless you want to use any of Titanium Backup's other features, which are numerous. If so, I suggest consulting the official documentation here:

http://www.titaniumtrack.com/kb/titanium-backup-kb

Sharing Your Internet Connection for Free With Wi-Fi Tether Router

Another advantage of rooting is that you can use a Wi-Fi tethering app without paying your carrier's hot spot fees.

WARNING: Although your carrier has no way of knowing with certainty that you are tethering, you will likely set off alarms if you use a massive amount of bandwidth. I advise against using this method to stream video or download large files. Use it for regular web browsing and you will be fine. Of course, I take no responsibility for your actions if you choose to violate the terms of your contract!

On many other recent Android phones, the Wi-Fi tethering app of choice has been Wi-Fi Tether-TrevE Mod. However, its developer has not updated it since April 2013, and the last version does not work with the Galaxy S5.

The best alternative at this time is an app in the Google Play Store called "WiFi Tether Router" ($2.50). Most users report it works well, and the developer has a reputation for responsiveness, so the risk is very minimal. It works well for me. Make sure you uncheck the box that the app instructs you to uncheck.

Do not buy WiFi Tether Router unless you have rooted your Galaxy S5. If you are not rooted, you will waste $2.50 and not be able to use the app.

Freezing Background Apps With Greenify to Save Battery Power

One longstanding problem with the Android OS is the way it handles apps running in the background. It tends to be far too permissive, allowing apps to send and receive data and keep your Galaxy S5's processor working, draining valuable battery power. Greenify solves these problems. Once installed and configures, it regularly freezes apps in the background so that they cannot affect your battery life. I notice a dramatic difference in my Galaxy S5's battery life when I enable Greenify, and it is one of my favorite apps.

To use Greenify, first download and install it from the Google Play Store. Open it and tap the plus (+) sign in the bottom-left-hand corner of the screen.

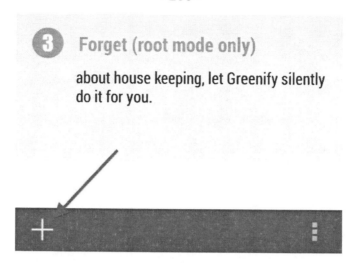

Tap "Show more apps" and then tap apps that you do not want to run in the background. Note that any apps you select will be completely frozen while operating in the background and will not be able to send you any notifications at all. For this reason, carefully select which apps you want to freeze. Once you have selected the apps you want to freeze, tap the checkmark in the upper-right-hand corner of the screen.

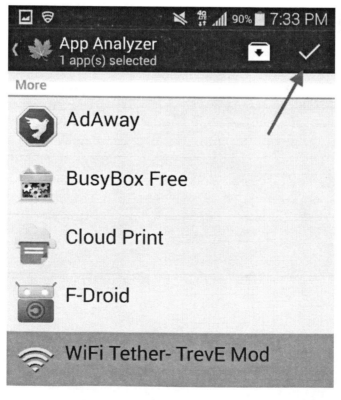

Then, if you install more apps in the future that you want to freeze, do so by tapping the plus sign along the bottom edge of Greenify's main screen.

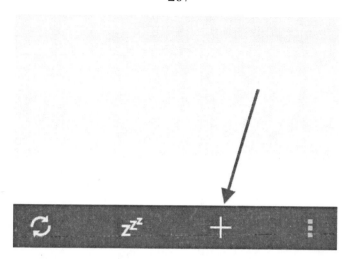

That's it! You will likely experience an appreciable improvement in your Galaxy S5's battery life. Remember to update Greenify periodically as you install new apps on your Galaxy S5.

Improving Multi Window

By default, Samsung has only enabled certain apps to run in Multi Window. By rooting your Galaxy S5 and installing a third-party utility, you can run any app you want in Multi Window.

To do this, first root your Galaxy S5 as described above. Second, download Multi Window Apps Manager by Aeon Time from the Google Play Store:

Open it, select the apps you wish to use in Multi Window, and tap the save (floppy disk) icon at the bottom of the screen. Reboot your Galaxy S5, and the changes will be made. Note that you will have to tap the small arrow at the bottom of the Multi Window panel, and then "Edit" to add apps you've enabled with Multi Window App Manager to the Multi Window Panel.

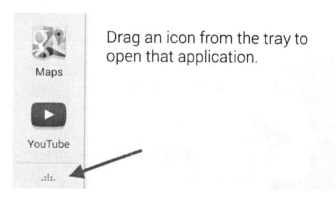

Drag an icon from the tray to open that application.

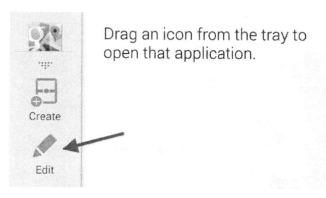

Drag an icon from the tray to open that application.

Create

Edit

Although most apps work fine in Multi Window mode, some may be buggy or cause your Galaxy S5 to slow down. If this happens, you can Google for a specific solution, but you are probably out of luck. However, the vast majority of apps work fine.

Using NFC Tags to Quickly Perform Tasks

One cool and little-known feature of the Galaxy S5 is its compatibility with Samsung's TecTiles 2 tags. These are tiny 1x1" stickers with embedded RFID chips. You can place them around your home, car, or office, and program them to do different tasks when you tap your Galaxy S5 on them. For example, you might stick one on your car's dashboard and program it to toggle GPS, open the Maps app, and start playing music.

You can buy TecTiles 2 from Samsung.com, Amazon.com, or similar online retailers.

To use TecTiles 2, download and install the Samsung TecTile app from the Google Play Store. Follow its instructions to program your TecTiles 2. Make sure NFC is turned on, or your Galaxy S5 will not detect TecTiles 2 tags when you tap it against them.

Personally, my most-used TecTile 2 is one on the wall next to my bed. I have a night and a normal profile, and my TecTile 2 switches between them. At night, I tap my Galaxy S5 to decrease the brightness, silence it, and open the Clock app so I can set an alarm. In the morning, I tap my Galaxy S5 on the same TecTile 2 to turn up the brightness, and turn my ringer on again.

Make sure you purchase TecTiles 2, not the original TecTiles. The originals are incompatible with the Galaxy S5.

Using a USB OTG Cable to Connect Keyboards, Mice, and USB Drives

USB OTG (On-The-Go) is another little-known feature of Android and is fully supported on the Galaxy S5. Purchase a USB OTG adapter like the one linked below, and you'll be able to connect USB flash drives, mice, keyboards, game controllers, and other accessories to your Galaxy S5. It is even possible to use USB OTG in conjunction with a USB hub, to connect multiple devices at the same time.

http://www.amazon.com/dp/B00871Q5PI

If connecting a USB drive, you will need to eject it before unplugging the USB OTG cable. To do so, swipe down the notification panel and tap the notification. Wait a few seconds until you see a confirmation message.

Installing Adobe Flash

Although Flash is slowly being phased out in favor of newer technologies like HTML5, it is still common enough that you might want it on your Galaxy S5. Flash is no longer in the Google Play Store, but you can download and install the last archived version directly from Adobe's site:

http://download.macromedia.com/pub/flashplayer/insta llers/archive/android/11.1.115.81/install_flash_player_ics. apk

(Short URL: http://goo.gl/AsLccx)

Neither Chrome nor the stock Internet browser support Flash, so you will need to download a third-party alternative. I recommend UC Browser, available free from the Google Play Store.

Saving Battery Power

At various points in this book, I have made suggestions about how to conserve battery power. Here, I will consolidate them all for you and provide some additional information.

In general, the greatest source of power consumption on Android devices is the screen. On the Galaxy S5, you will notice a massive difference in battery life depending on the brightness setting you use. If you're having battery life woes, this is the first thing to check. I find that on the Galaxy S5, even 20% brightness is more than enough for comfortable usage except in bright sunlight.

> The Galaxy S5 has a Super AMOLED screen, which does not have a backlight—rather, the brightness of each individual pixel is individually controlled. This means that it takes less power to display darker colors. One trick to reduce your screen's power consumption is to use dark wallpaper and set apps to use dark themes when possible.

The second greatest source of battery drain is apps themselves. In general, you will notice your battery life decline as you install more apps—and to some degree, this is normal. If you are installing apps that perform background services, which many do, they will use some power.

However, many apps are poorly coded and drain much more than their fair share of battery power. Try to only install reputable apps, and if your battery is draining faster than it should, uninstall or disable apps you're not using. If you root your Galaxy S5 (p. 255), install Greenify (p. 265) to completely freeze background apps. Greenify is amazing for improving your battery life.

You can view estimates of battery usage by app in system settings → Battery. If you are having a serious problem and can't seem to find the culprit, your only option may be to factory reset your Galaxy S5 and install apps a couple at a time until you identify the offender.

Here are some additional ways to reclaim battery life:

- Swipe down the notification panel with two fingers to access the extended toggle buttons (p. 56), and enable Power Saving Mode or Ultra Power Saving Mode (p. 234).

- Use Wi-Fi instead of cellular networks when possible; the Wi-Fi radio requires much less power. Some people think that turning Wi-Fi off saves battery life throughout the day. This is not true. If you are connected to a Wi-Fi network, your Galaxy S5 will consume less power than if you were connected to a 4G LTE network.

- Delete unused widgets from your home screens and disable unused features in system settings.

- Don't set up a Samsung account; it uses a fair amount of battery power and provides few to no real benefits. If you have one, delete it in system settings → Accounts.

- Enable Music Auto Off in the Music app (if you use it).

- Disable "Location" in the notification panel when you don't need GPS or other location detection.

- For apps that regularly connect to the Internet, check their settings menus to see if you can reduce the frequency with which they check for updates.

- Buy a high-capacity aftermarket battery and back cover from a site like Amazon.com. Or, buy an additional Samsung battery. Read about these options in Chapter 10 (p. 297).

- In really tight situations, press and hold the power button, and then tap "Emergency mode (p. 35)." The functionality of your S5 will be greatly reduced, but your battery life will be extended as much as possible.

> Advanced users may want to check out BetterBatteryStats ($2.89 on the Google Play Store). It has a steep learning curve beyond the scope of this book, but is a very powerful tool for determining what is draining your battery.

Keeping Your Battery Healthy

To make your battery last as long as possible in the long run, try to run it down to ~10% every couple weeks—but try not to go much lower, and if you must, charge it up as soon as possible thereafter. It's okay to run it down to 10% more often— just don't let it drain all the way and sit idle for an extended period of time, because doing so will eventually ruin your battery. If you treat you battery properly, it should last for as long as you own your Galaxy S5.

> Use the included charger to charge the Galaxy S5 when possible, as it outputs much more current than most smartphones' chargers. However, contrary to some reports on the Internet, it is not necessary to use a USB 3.0 cable to achieve maximum charging speed. A USB 2.0 cable will charge your Galaxy S5 just as quickly, as long as it's connected to the appropriate charger. Note that charging via a computer's USB port *will* take much longer than with the included charger.

Online Resources / Getting Help With Your Galaxy S5

There are numerous Android-related online communities, but two of my favorites are Android Central and XDA. Android Central is an excellent source of Android news and reviews, while XDA is my preferred source for all things related to rooting and customization. The site has dedicated forums for each of the major carriers:

> **Sprint: http://forum.xda-developers.com/sprint-galaxy-s5**
>
> **T-Mobile: http://forum.xda-developers.com/tmobile-galaxy-s5**
>
> **Verizon: http://forum.xda-developers.com/verizon-galaxy-s5**
>
> **AT&T: http://forum.xda-developers.com/att-galaxy-s5**

Either of these websites is a good place to ask for help with your Galaxy S5—but in my experience, XDA is a better place to seek help with more technical issues.

Chapter 8: What Do These Apps Do?

Good work. By now, you know more about the Galaxy S5 than 99% of other users—but we're not done yet.

In this chapter, I give you a quick rundown of several preloaded apps whose functionality may not be immediately obvious. I tell you what each one does—often it is unclear without experimentation—and give you my commentary on its overall usefulness and potential alternatives. The Galaxy S5 includes some very good and interesting apps, but it also includes some "bloatware," junk apps that Samsung gets paid to include but are not the best options out there. (Though, it contains much less bloatware than previous Galaxy S models.)

For apps that I discuss at length elsewhere in the book, I link you to the relevant discussion.

Amazon

Samsung has preloaded the Amazon app on the Galaxy S5. Normally, I'd complain about a shopping app being preloaded on my phone, but come on... it's Amazon! Can't complain too much about that.

The Amazon app is actually one of the best e-commerce apps available for Android. It's fast, responsive, and unlike many of its competitors, it isn't missing any features. In many ways, it's actually superior to browsing Amazon on the web due to its streamlined interface, and I frequently use the app when placing orders with Amazon.

Note that the Amazon app is not for reading Kindle books. For that, you must download the "Amazon Kindle" app from the Google Play store.

ChatON

ChatON is Samsung's proprietary messaging app. It allows you to message other ChatON users without burning through your SMS limit.

The app itself is not badly designed, and the concept is certainly welcome for users with a limited text messaging plan. The fatal flaw is its user base—your friends probably won't have it. Try more mainstream options such as WhatsApp (p. 295) from the Google Play Store. These apps do the same thing as ChatON but it's a lot more likely your friends will have them, too.

Drive/Dropbox

Google Drive and Dropbox are cloud storage apps that are both compatible with multiple platforms including Windows, Mac OS, and Android. They allow you to upload, backup, and download files to and from a virtual hard disk and synchronize your files across multiple devices. Google Drive's web interface also allows you to view and edit Microsoft Office documents.

Although I personally use Dropbox, Google Drive is a strong up-and-coming competitor. Google gives you much more free storage (15 GB vs. 2 GB) and its paid storage options are much cheaper ($2/month for 100 GB). I am planning to switch to Google Drive soon.

In general, I am a huge advocate of cloud storage services. I use Dropbox extensively and save all of my personal and work files to my Dropbox while using my PC. This way, I always have them available on my Galaxy S5.

In addition to keeping your files backed up and available on the cloud, Dropbox also saves every single version of your files—so you can revert to previous versions if you lose data. This has been invaluable for me and many other users.

If you aren't using one of these services, pick one—my suggestion is Google Drive even though I'm still on Dropbox—and start using it right away. You'll never look back.

Flipboard/My Magazine

Flipboard is a content aggregator, combining news and social media feeds to create a personalized 'magazine.'

Flipboard has a very strong following and many users love it. Personally, it never really grew on me and I find its flashy interface to be too distracting. When I read news, I just want to get straight to the information, and raw text works the best for me. I use gReader (p. 286). Also, Flipboard loses some of its value if you are not a big social media user since social network integration is a central feature. Flipboard is a love-it-or-hate-it app.

Flipboard is very similar to My Magazine, which you can access by swiping all the way to the left on the home screen.

Google

If you have enabled Google Now, this will open it. If you have not, it will simply open a Google search utility.

I have never found a need to use this app shortcut. When I want to search Google, I simply open Chrome and search. When I want to access Google Now, I hold the home key.

Google Settings

Google Settings allows you to customize a few Android-related options in your Google account, right on your Galaxy S5.

It is helpful to be aware of the settings in this app, although you will probably only rarely use it, if ever. If you want to investigate all of the options available in your Google account, you'll want to use this desktop site instead of the limited app.

https://www.google.com/dashboard

Google+

Google+ is the mobile client for Google's social network alternative to Facebook. It will let you interact with other users (friends, family, etc.) who also use Google+.

If you are among the select group of Google+ enthusiasts, this is the only app in town. If you're new to social networks in general, you'll probably want to look at Facebook before Google+, because it has a much, much larger user base. I have resisted using Google+ because Google has pushed it in ways I don't like, such as trying to force users to use their real names as YouTube screen names through Google+.

Hangouts

Hangouts is the mobile client for Google's chat platform—the same one you see when you're logged into Gmail. It replaced Google Talk in 2013.

Hangouts is a fine app and Google has put a lot of effort into improving it since it came out. It does not significantly drain your battery while running and works very well for text or video chatting with your contacts. If you use Gmail chat a lot, Hangouts is the best program for doing so on your Galaxy S5.

Lookout Security

Lookout does three main things: 1) protects you from viruses and malware, 2) backs up your Google contacts and photos, and 3) allows you to locate your phone by GPS if you lose it.

In my opinion, Lookout is a good app but it's bloated. The backup function is redundant, because your Google contacts are already automatically backed up with Google. And, you can easily use a feature like Dropbox's Camera Upload to back up your photos plus sync them with your desktop or laptop computer. Also, if you want the full range of features from Lookout, you'll have to pay a monthly fee of $3.

Personally, I use an app called Cerberus (p. 283) instead of Lookout. It has even more powerful remote location and wiping features, but it does not have antivirus features. If this is a deal breaker for you, Lookout is a better option. Personally, I avoid viruses by sticking to trusted app developers and not downloading unknown email attachments. Using these techniques, I have never had a virus problem in all my years of using Android devices.

Memo

Memo is a very simple notepad app. It can handle text, images, and voice attachments. Personally, I use Evernote (p. 285) instead, which has a PC/Mac OSX client and automatically backs up notes to the cloud. If you're serious about note taking, forget the Memo app and look into Evernote.

My Files

My Files is a file manager. It lets you access the file system of your Galaxy S5 and your SD card.

My Files works fine but it is inferior and limited compared to the excellent and free ES File Explorer (p. 284). ES File Explorer has a better interface, allows root access to file directories, and is frequently updated. Ditch My Files and don't look back. The one exception is that you'll need to use My Files to view files you've hidden using Private Mode (p. 211).

Photos

The Photos app sets up a service that automatically backs up your camera photos to your Google+ account. But don't worry—no one can see them on Google+ until you manually share them. Unlike the Gallery app, its main function is not to view media.

Overall, I really like the idea of this app. It's no fun (to say the least) to lose your photos, and a cloud backup option like this is a great way to prevent loss. Personally, I use the Camera Upload feature of Dropbox to accomplish the same thing, but the Photos app is a fine alternative if you don't use Dropbox.

Play Books/Games/Movies & TV/Music/Newsstand

This is a group of apps that complement the Play Store. They allow you to buy and consume media (movies, music, books, magazines, etc.) from Google.

All of these apps work well, have reasonable prices, and have a large selection. Whether you use them or not will likely depend on the degree to which you've already bought into other platforms. For example, I read all of my eBooks on my Kindle, so I buy eBooks exclusively from Amazon and never from Play Books. Similarly, if you are already invested in iTunes, you might not want to buy music from Google Music. But if you're not already invested anywhere else, Google Play is not a bad platform on which to invest in a media collection.

POLARIS Office 5

POLARIS Office 5 is a Microsoft Office-compatible productivity suite. It includes Word, Excel, and PowerPoint functionality.

There are a lot of Office-compatible suites for Android. POLARIS works well in general and is free—you probably won't need anything more for light or occasional document viewing. If you plan to edit extensively and/or need to edit complex documents, you might need to try other Office apps to find the one that works best for your particular needs. You can try Google's Quickoffice (free), Microsoft Office Mobile (free, and particularly good at preserving document formatting), or OfficeSuite Pro 7 ($14.99 in the Google Play Store and highly rated by critics).

See more information on POLARIS here (p. 245).

S Health

S Health offers several tools to track and maintain your fitness, including a pedometer, a GPS tracker for running, a food tracker, a weight diary, and more.

S Health is worth a shot if you're trying to improve your fitness. It is missing some advanced features found in products like the Fitbit One such as sleep tracking, but the price is right. This is likely a niche app, but it is worth trying if you think it could help you.

See more information on S Health here (p. 240).

S Voice

S Voice is Samsung's voice command system. It offers most of the same commands as Google Now, but unlike Google Now does not have a card system.

I was extremely surprised at how well S Voice performed during my testing. Although its voice recognition is slower than Google Now's, it was more accurate for me and handled my requests just as well if not better. For users who do not like the proactive card system of Google Now, S Voice is a solid alternative. My guess is that Google Now has more long term potential because it's backed by the power of Google itself, but for the time being, S Voice is not bad at all. I strongly suggest you give it a spin and see whether it works better for you than Google Now.

See more information on S Voice here (p. 180).

Samsung Apps

Samsung Apps is Samsung's proprietary app store—a competitor to the Google Play Store.

I suggest avoiding Samsung Apps completely. Once in a while you can find apps cheaper in Samsung Apps than the Play Store, but the selection of apps is no contest. Additionally, if you buy apps through Samsung Apps, you won't be able to install them on future non-Samsung Androids that you own. Not a great trade-off.

The one exception is if you need to download Samsung apps like the Galaxy Gear Manager. In this case, you have no option but to use Samsung Apps, because many Samsung-specific apps aren't available in the Google Play Store.

Smart Remote

Smart Remote is a universal TV remote control that takes advantage of the Galaxy S5's built-in IR blaster.

In my tests, Smart Remote worked well with my Panasonic plasma television. There are a few random IR remote control alternatives on the Google Play Store, but Smart Remote works very well and is free. Smart Remote adds real value to the Galaxy S5.

Voice Search

Voice Search is Google's voice search utility. Not only does it let you search Google using your voice, but it also accepts any and all commands that work in Google Now. In my opinion, it's easier just to tap and hold the home button.

YouTube

YouTube allows you to watch YouTube videos on your Galaxy S5.

For the most part, the YouTube app is very well designed and has the same functionality as the desktop version. However, in some cases, certain videos are inexplicably not available on mobile devices. Still, it's the only game in town. If you want to download YouTube videos for later use, try an app such as TubeMate.

http://tubemate.net/

Chapter 9: The 50 All-Time Best Android Apps

Below is a list of my all-time best app recommendations, taken from my book, *The 50 All-Time Best Android Apps*. Some are free and some are paid. I am in no way affiliated with any of the developers, and I stand to gain nothing from your purchases. My recommendations come from my own experience and research. http://www.amazon.com/dp/B00L8ES1L2

1Weather

1Weather is an attractive, functional weather app. It contains all the weather information you need, including hourly, daily, and weekly forecasts. It also offers real-time weather mapping, sunrise/sunset information, and push notifications to keep you informed of changing conditions. Plus, you can easily switch between cities when you travel. In my opinion, no other Android weather app comes close to 1Weather's functionality, style, and simplicity.

Price: Free from the Google Play Store / $1.99 in-app purchase to remove ads

AirDroid

AirDroid offers a unique way to control your Android device—using a web browser on your desktop or laptop computer. After you have installed the app on your Android, you just go to http://web.airdroid.com/ in your browser to open the control panel. From there, you can view photos and videos, change your ringtone, manage contacts, send and receive text messages, listen to music on your Android device, transfer files, take screenshots, and more.

In this way, AirDroid is good for many purposes—mass updates of your phone book with the convenience of a keyboard, showing photos on a big screen, transferring files wirelessly instead of over a USB cable, texting on your computer, and more. Plus, it's totally free!

Price: Free from the Google Play Store

Amazon Appstore

Although most apps on the Amazon Appstore can also be found on the Google Play Store, the Amazon Appstore has some important advantages. First, Amazon offers a free app every day. Sometimes the free apps are excellent—for example, I've gotten several office suites for free over the years. Free games are also common. Second, apps sometimes go on sale on the Amazon Appstore but not on the Google Play Store.

The only catch is that if you install apps from the Amazon Appstore and subsequently uninstall the Amazon Appstore itself, those apps will stop working. Simple solution: don't uninstall the Amazon Appstore. After all, you'll need it to check the free app of the day.

Price: Free from http://www.amazon.com/gp/mas/get/android

Authenticator

Google Authenticator is a two-factor security solution that works with many websites that require a password login, including Gmail, Dropbox, Dashlane (p. 284), and Evernote (p. 285).

What is a two-factor security solution?

With Authenticator, anyone who logs into your (Gmail, Dropbox, Dashlane, Evernote, etc.) account will be required to input a code generated by Authenticator *in addition* to the password. This way, even if someone steals your password, they will not be able to log into your account without also having physical possession of your Android. Authenticator even works when your device has no Internet connection. The biggest downside is that only certain websites and software support it.

Price: Free from the Google Play Store

Barcode Scanner

Barcode Scanner allows you to scan barcodes and QR codes. I use it to comparison shop at the store, to quickly pull up reviews of products, and to scan QR codes in viral advertisements. Barcode Scanner also happens to be required for some features in Authenticator.

Price: Free from the Google Play Store

Boson X

Boson X is one of the few Android games that has stood the test of time for me. It is a unique, arcade-style game with a fantastic soundtrack. It is easy to pick up and play when you only have a few minutes to kill, but deep enough to keep you occupied for hours if you want. Not many games strike this balance as well as Boson X.

Price: $2.99 from the Google Play Store

Call Recorder

Have you ever wanted to record voice calls on your Android phone? Although quite expensive at $9.95, Call Recorder by skvalex is the best call recording app available and is capable of recording to both WAV and MP3. Plus, root access is not required for most phones. But before recording any calls, make sure you're aware of the wiretapping laws in your jurisdiction.

Price: Free trial from http://goo.gl/u690rm / $9.95 to buy on the Google Play Store

Cerberus Anti Theft

Most "Best App" lists say that Lookout is the best Android anti theft app available, but I disagree. Cerberus is my security app of choice. Unlike Lookout and most other phone-locating security apps, Cerberus has absolutely no monthly fee—only a one-time purchase of $4. Better yet, it doesn't slow down your phone, doesn't drain your battery, works reliably, and can even hide itself from the app drawer. Its online control panel is simple and streamlined and works every time. I trust Cerberus more than any other app to help me retrieve my Android smartphone should I ever lose it.

Price: Free trial from the Google Play Store / $4 to buy

Chipotle

No, this is not a joke! For a long time, Chipotle only had an iOS app, and they did a poor job of announcing the Android app when they finally released it in late 2013, so I want to spread the word. The app is well-designed, easy to use, and most importantly, allows you to order online and go straight to the register to pick up your order. No more waiting in line. Oh, yeah. Any app that can save 20-30 minutes of my day is a winner. If you don't eat at Chipotle but you do eat at other quick serve restaurants, see if they have a similar app on the Google Play store that will allow you to skip the line. Many do.

Price: Free from the Google Play Store

Chrome to Phone

Chrome to Phone is an app & browser extension combo that lets you instantly send links and text from your desktop browser to your Android device. You must install both the app on your Android and the Chrome extension on your computer. Once installed, just click the Chrome to Phone button in your browser to send the current tab to Chrome on your mobile device. You can also highlight text on your computer, right click, and select "Chrome to Phone" to copy it to your Android's clipboard. It's a very convenient way to quickly get needed information to your Android device.

Price: Free from the Google Play Store

Cloud Print

Want to wirelessly print from your Android device? Cloud Print is a brand new official Google app that lets you do exactly that. You just install a Chrome extension on your desktop or laptop computer, register your printer with Google Cloud Print, install the Android app, and you're set. No printer drivers or complicated wireless settings needed. The Android app lets you print documents, photos, PDFs, and more. You can also print directly from mobile Chrome.

Price: Free from the Google Play Store

Dashlane

Dashlane is a cross-platform password manager. I use it extensively on my desktop to autofill personal information and credit card numbers, generate random passwords, and store my login info for everything. The Android client is a must-have because it makes all your passwords available on the go. If you are looking for a password manager, I highly recommend Dashlane. The Android client isn't perfect (they're still working on autofill for Android) but the overall experience is excellent. I have tried alternatives such as LastPass, and I always come back to Dashlane for its bug-free functionality and clean interface.

Price: Desktop client is free from https://www.dashlane.com, Android client is free from the Google Play Store; subscription (which is necessary for cloud syncing to Android) is $29.99/year

eBay

eBay's mobile app is free and much better than its slow and buggy mobile website. In the past, the official app was actually inferior to a third-party app called Pocket Auctions, but it's come a long way since then. It supports all major features, including search filters, best offers, PayPal payments, and so on. If you're a regular eBay user, get it now. You'll also want to grab the free PayPal app for additional PayPal features beyond auction payments.

Price: Free from the Google Play Store

ES File Explorer

ES File Explorer is a full-featured file manager. Although Androids do not prominently feature a file and folder storage system like on PCs, these things do exist behind the scenes, and ES File Explorer lets you access them. It is much more powerful than the "My Files" app that comes with most Android devices, and I recommend it wholeheartedly for copying, moving, renaming, and deleting files saved on your internal memory or your external SD card. If you've rooted your device, it can also access read-only system partitions.

Price: Free from the Google Play Store

Evernote

Evernote is a cross-platform cloud note-taking app, and supports both Windows and MacOS in addition to Android. How many of us just email notes to ourselves, or scrawl them on the backs of napkins? Evernote is a much easier and more secure way of keeping notes organized and synchronized between devices. Any note you save into Evernote is automatically backed up in the cloud and copied to your other devices, so you'll never lose data or be without your notes. I use Evernote for shopping lists, journaling, organizing notes for my books, brainstorming, and more. And unless you store a ton of images or audio recordings in your notes, you'll be totally fine with the free service.

Price: Free trial from the Google Play Store; desktop version available at https://evernote.com / Premium service $5 per month

Google Drive

Google Drive is so much more than a simple app. Drive gives you cloud storage space, where you can upload and store files from your computer or mobile device. (And if you weren't already aware, you already have a Drive account if you have a Gmail account. Access it at http://drive.google.com.)

The benefits of using Drive are threefold. First, any files saved on your Drive are backed up. If your computer hard drive crashes or you lose your Android device, any files saved to your Drive will survive. Second, since you can access Drive via your computer or the app on your Android, your files are available no matter where you are. Forget to email yourself a file? No problem—as long as your desktop computer has the Drive software installed and you saved the file to your Drive, you can get it with the Android app. Third, Drive saves every version of every file. Accidentally overwrite your thesis? Just log into the web interface and roll back the file.

Personally, I have the Windows/Mac desktop Drive software *and* the mobile app, and I save all my work files to my Drive folder. This way, I never lose data and I am never without my data.

In the past, I recommended Dropbox instead of Drive. However, Google now offers significantly more free space than Dropbox (15 GB vs. 2 GB), and its paid plans are significantly cheaper (100 GB for $1.99/month vs. $9.99/month.) If you aren't already using Drive, start today.

Price: Free from the Google Play Store

gReader

gReader is an RSS reader that synchronizes with a Feedly account to bring all your news to your Android device. If you aren't familiar with RSS feeds, here's what you need to know: Most news websites and blogs publish them. RSS feeds are files that syndicate all the posts from their respective websites. When you import them into an RSS reader like Feedly, they let you read news from multiple sources all in one place without visiting many different websites, which is fast and convenient. gReader is simply an app for using your Feedly account on your Android device.

If you want the best-looking RSS app, you might prefer the official Feedly app, Pulse, or Flipboard. But for a functional, no-nonsense RSS reader with plenty of functions like offline reading, gReader is the way to go. There is a free version, but the paid version removes ads and provides extra features like better widgets and voice reading of articles.

Price: Free trial from the Google Play Store / $4.69 to buy

GTasks

Many Android devices do not come with a good to-do app, and where those apps do exist, they generally don't sync with Google Tasks. GTasks is a simple to-do list that solves this problem. If you want a simple to-do list that you can access from both your Android and your Gmail account on your computer, GTasks is the way to go. It has a nice, simple interface, and it has never failed to save and synchronize my tasks.

Price: Free trial from the Google Play Store / $4.99 to buy

Key Ring Reward Cards & Coupon

Key Ring stores all of your loyalty and shopping rewards cards. Don't let those frequent flyer miles go to waste! Better yet, it allows you to easily share cards with other Key Ring users and access weekly fliers and coupons that cashiers can scan right from your phone's screen. The one downside is the in-app ads, and there is no premium version to remove them.

Price: Free from the Google Play Store

Kitchen Timer

Kitchen Timer corrects the one-timer-at-a-time deficiency found in most stock Clock apps. Kitchen Timer allows you to set up to three timers at once and doesn't require any unusual installation privileges. It's a great, bare-bones app and is completely free. I use it all the time when I'm cooking two dishes at once.

Price: Free from the Google Play Store

MX Player

MX Player is my favorite video player. Your Android's built-in Video app is probably sufficient if you only watch short clips, but if you watch a lot of movies, TV shows, or files in obscure formats, MX Player will provide a much better experience. It also handles subtitles like a champ. The paid version removes ads.

Price: Free trial from the Google Play Store / CA~$6.00 to buy

Mycelium Bitcoin Wallet

If you don't know what Bitcoin is, you can skip this app. If you do, all you need to know is that Mycelium is the best Bitcoin wallet for Android. It has features that other apps don't, such as full BIP38 paper wallet support, and it's open source so you can be confident it's safe to use. I always keep some bitcoin in my Mycelium wallet in case I stumble upon a store or restaurant that accepts it.

Price: Free from the Google Play Store

Netflix

If you have a Netflix subscription, the Netflix app is a must-have. If you don't have a Netflix subscription, what are you thinking?!? Netflix is one of the best consumer services in today's economy, period. The value is... amazing. Get a subscription so you can watch amazing video like Breaking Bad, House of Cards, Sherlock, Law & Order, and more.

Price: Free from the Google Play Store (Netflix streaming subscription required)

Nova Launcher

Nova Launcher is a highly customizable home screen replacement. If you're tired of the stock look of your device (Samsung TouchWiz, HTC Sense, etc.), then try Nova Launcher. You can customize the number of rows and columns for the apps displayed on each screen, margins, scroll effects, shadows, your app tray, and much more. You can even hide apps from your app drawer.

Price: Free trial from the Google Play Store / $4.00 to buy

Office Suite 7 Pro

Office Suite 7 Pro is an excellent, feature-packed office suite for Android. It is fast, highly compatible, and has a great user interface. Many users believe it is unquestionably the best Microsoft Office replacement for Android. It's not cheap, but if you wait until a major holiday to buy it, you can sometimes get it on sale for $9.99 or less from Google Play and/or the Amazon Appstore. I especially recommend Office Suite 7 Pro if you're a heavy Microsoft Office user and/or you want the best preservation of your documents' formatting. If you are only a casual Microsoft Office user, take a look at Google's free office suite, Quickoffice (p. 289), instead.

Price: Free 7-day trial from the Google Play Store / $14.99 to buy

Pandora

Pandora is a music-streaming service. Its library of songs is much smaller than Spotify's (p. 292) and it doesn't let you play specific songs, but it's a great resource for discovering new music similar to what you already like. I don't pull up Pandora when I want to hear a specific song, but rather when I want to hear something new. Pandora is free, but you can only skip 6 songs per hour and you will have to endure ads unless you pay for the premium service. I don't really recommend subscribing, though—your money is much better spent with Spotify. Take what you get from Pandora's free service and run with it.

Price: Free from the Google Play Store / subscription service $4.99 per month

PayPal

If you use PayPal for personal payments or business, the Android app is a must-have. It's much faster and easier than using the full PayPal site on a mobile browser and supports most common functions. (Though, it does not have the ability to create a custom invoice, which I would like to see added.) I use it to square up restaurant checks with friends and family, to make online purchases, and to collect money for my business.

Price: Free from the Google Play Store

Play Music

Although Google Play Music is not the best standalone MP3 player on Android (that title belongs to Poweramp, in my opinion), the other features of the Play Music ecosystem nevertheless make it the best way to listen to your music collection on the go. Why? Google allows you to upload up to 20,000 of your own songs to the cloud—for free—which are then available to stream from your Android via the Play Music app, from your web browser, or from any public computer. This allows you to have your entire music collection available on-demand through your Android, without requiring any storage space. But don't worry—if you want to download music for offline playback, Play Music makes that easy, too. Overall, Play Music is an amazing and free service, and is the absolute best way to take your music collection with you.

Price: Free from the Google Play Store / Download desktop Music Manager   from https://support.google.com/googleplay/answer/1229970?hl=en

Pocket Casts

Pocket Casts is, in my opinion, the best podcast app for Android. It does a magnificent job of managing, filtering, downloading, and playing your podcasts, and can even back up your settings to the cloud. Plus, it's really nice to look at.

Price: $3.99 on the Google Play Store

Quickoffice

Quickoffice is Google's free office suite, and is capable of both editing and creating Word, Excel, and PowerPoint files. It has tight integration with

Quickoffice, so it makes it easy to save/backup all your documents to your Google Drive account. If you are a casual Microsoft Office user, Quickoffice will be all you need on your Android. However, if you are a heavy Office user or you need the best possible preservation of your documents' formatting, you might want to take a look at Office Suite 7 Pro (p. 288) instead of Quickoffice.

Price: Free from the Google Play Store

RealCalc

RealCalc has a nicer interface than most stock Calculator apps and offers scientific functions. It also supports RPN mode and allows for a great deal of customization. The paid version adds more features such as fraction conversions, landscape mode, and support for degrees and minutes. It's my preferred Android calculator app.

Price: Free trial from the Google Play Store / $3.49 to buy

Reddit is Fun

If you read Reddit, I highly recommend Reddit is Fun. It's a much better way to browse Reddit than using a mobile browser and has all the features you could possibly want. There are a few other Reddit readers on the Google Play Store, but in my experience Reddit is Fun is the best of them.

Price: Free trial from the Google Play Store / $1.99 to buy

Ringtone Maker

Ringtone Maker does exactly what it sounds like: it allows you to edit MP3s and other audio files to create custom ringtones and easily assign them to contacts on your phone. It is much easier to use Ringtone Maker's all-in-one package than to try to use a separate music editor and figure out how to set the resulting file as a ringtone in OS settings. Ringtone Maker is absolutely free and adds a feature that should be, but rarely is, included by default on Android smartphones.

Price: Free from the Google Play Store

Scanner Radio

This app is awesome. It allows you to live stream police and emergency services radio frequencies to your Android. If you are in close proximity to an emergency response, you often can tune into the local frequencies and find out what's going on first-hand. Sometimes, you can even hear foot chases and other criminal pursuits as they happen.

Price: Free trial from the Google Play Store / $2.99 to buy

Screen Adjuster

Screen Adjuster is a small, free app that allows you to set your screen's brightness below the normal minimum level. It's very useful in dark environments to avoid losing your night vision or to avoid distracting others in public venues like movie theaters. Personally, I use it before bed to minimize the impact of my Android's screen on my melatonin levels. Science!

Price: Free trial from the Google Play Store / $0.99 to buy

Shazam

Shazam uses your Android's microphone to look up the artist/name of a song. It's like Google, but for music. Depending on the audio quality and background noise, it will listen for about 5-15 seconds before telling you what you're listening to. It's very accurate and has an extensive database; very rarely does it fail to identify a song. The paid version, called Shazam Encore, removes banner advertisements.

Price: Free trial from the Google Play Store / $5.59 to buy

SMS Backup & Restore

This app allows you to backup and restore your SMS and MMS messages to your SD card or Dropbox. It works seamlessly and quickly unlike many other text message backup apps. I highly recommend using it to back up your messages or to transfer them to a new phone.

Price: Free trial from the Google Play Store / $3.49 to buy

Snes9xEX+

This app is an excellent and free Super Nintendo emulator. After you have downloaded ROM game files from the Internet, you can load them into SNES9xEX+ and play them exactly as they were on the original console. (Legal caveat: you must own the original cartridges to legally download ROM files.) Remember Super Mario World, Zelda, and Final Fantasy II/III? Great games—play them with Snes9xEx+.

The author of Snes9xEx+, Robert Broglia, sells emulators for most other classic gaming consoles as well. Snes9xEx+ is the free one that hooks you; the rest cost money, but are all excellent apps.

Price: Free from the Google Play Store

Speedtest

Speedtest is a free app that tests the speed of your Internet connection, be it Wi-Fi or cellular. It's useful to help diagnose connectivity problems, or just to show your friends how much faster your 4G LTE cell connection is than their home broadband.

Price: Free from the Google Play Store

Spotify

Spotify is a streaming music app that competes with Pandora. Unlike Pandora, however, it allows you to select one artist and listen exclusively to them for free on shuffle mode. (For the smartphone app, that is; the desktop and tablet apps actually allow you to pick any song you want at any time—even without a subscription—but with advertisements.) If you want to select songs individually on the Android smartphone app, you have to pay for the premium service. Spotify is a great complement to Pandora and has a huge library of songs (there's not much you won't find on it). If you subscribe to one streaming service, Spotify gets my vote. I have a subscription to it.

Price: Free from the Google Play Store / subscription service $9.99 per month

SuperBeam

SuperBeam is the best way to perform blazing-fast, wireless file transfers between Android devices. SuperBeam uses Wi-Fi Direct but implements it a lot more effectively than the Android OS does. When two Android phones have SuperBeam installed, they are on the same page—end of story. There's no messing around with complicated device settings like Android Beam, Wi-Fi Direct, or S Beam. I strongly recommend you use SuperBeam to transfer large files between Android devices.

Price: Free trial from the Google Play Store / $1.99 to buy

Talon for Twitter

Talon is an up-and-coming Twitter client that I like better than the official app and the other alternatives on the Google Play Store. It has great developer support, multi-account support, and costs less than $2.

Price: $1.99 from the Google Play Store

Tapatalk

If you read or participate in any online discussion forums, Tapatalk is an absolute must-have app. It condenses forum interfaces into a mobile-friendly format, and makes it much easier to read and post from your Android device. It's kind of like an RSS reader, but for forums. Tapatalk is probably one of my most-used apps—in fact, I would even use a desktop version if they made it. Nearly all major online discussion forums support Tapatalk as of 2014.

Price: Free trial from the Google Play Store / $2.99 to buy

TeamViewer

TeamViewer is a cross-platform screen-sharing program. You set up the client on your desktop computer and then access and control it from your Android phone. **Yes, this means you can control your computer's screen right from your Android device!** It works very well, even over slower connections. TeamViewer is incredibly cool and useful, and best of all, it's completely free for personal use.

Price: Free from the Google Play Store; desktop client available at http://www.teamviewer.com/

TeslaLED

TeslaLED is a free flashlight program that is much brighter than most built-in flashlight apps. It includes several handy widgets for quickly turning your Android's camera flash LED into a flashlight. I also really like that it doesn't request any unusual permissions at installation.

Price: Free from the Google Play Store / $1.00 optional donation

TinyShark Downloader

TinyShark Downloader lets you search for music on Grooveshark and download it to your Android device in MP3 format for playback on the music player of your choice (I suggest Google Play Music (p. 289); see above). I haven't found an easier way to search for and download MP3s. Of course, be sure to only download songs to which you are legally entitled.

Price: Free from http://exigocs.com/

TouchDown For Smartphones

TouchDown is the best Microsoft Outlook replacement, bar none. It has all the built-in features of Outlook including Mail, Calendar, Tasks, and so on. If your work uses Exchange, TouchDown is simply an excellent way to keep up with your work on the go. Moreover, because it consolidates all the functions of Outlook into a single app, it creates a very nice barrier between your work life and your personal life. It's not cheap, but if you use Outlook, it's well worth it.

Price: Free trial from the Google Play Store / $19.99 to buy

TuneIn Radio

This app allows you to stream local and national AM/FM radio stations over the Internet. It's very useful for listening to radio stations in other parts of the country, for example while traveling. It can also be useful for tuning in to local stations when your regular radio reception is poor but you have a good Internet connection.

Price: Free trial from the Google Play Store / $3.99 to buy

WhatsApp Messenger

Don't have unlimited texts? No problem. Get WhatsApp and get your friends to do the same. It uses a proprietary network to send and receives text-based messages without burning through your SMS quota. There are a lot of services like WhatsApp, but it has my recommendation because it is the most popular one and your friends and family are more likely to already have it.

Price: Free from the Google Play Store

ZArchiver

ZArchiver is an archive manager compatible with a huge array of file types, including .zip, .rar, .7z, and many, many more. It is very fast, lightweight, and completely free.

Price: Free from the Google Play Store / $1.30 optional donation

BONUS: The 8 All-Time Best Root Apps

If you read Android news or discussion forums online, you are probably familiar with the term "rooting." If not, let me briefly explain.

On any Linux-based operating system, including Android, the root user is the most privileged user account on the machine and can run code that requires special administrator authorization. The root account is not normally accessible to the user. "Rooting" your Android is a procedure that allows your device to override this limitation and run code as the root user. Once rooted, you can install and use some apps that are not normally possible to use. There are thousands of root apps available, but here is a quick bonus list of my top 8:

Greenify: One flaw of Android compared to iOS is that background apps can seriously drain your battery even when you're not using them. (iOS deals with background apps in a different way that prevents this issue.) Greenify allows you to freeze these apps and reclaim battery life. If you have a lot of apps installed, you'll be amazed how much your battery life improves with Greenify.

Titanium Backup: Titanium Backup allows you to back up your apps and data to your SD card. This is useful because you can restore apps much faster from an SD card than from the Google Play Store, something that you need to do each time you install a new custom ROM while rooted. Titanium Backup has been around forever, has good developer support, and has my recommendation.

AdAway: Available from the F-Droid app repository, AdAway blocks all ads on your device. This includes ads on web pages and inside apps. It is an absolute must-have.

ROM Toolbox Pro: This app gives you several important root utilities, such as reboot to recovery and a build.prop editor. You'll eventually want or need to do these things if you root, and ROM Toolbox Pro is a great way to do them.

BetterBatteryStats: This app has unparalleled power to help you figure out the source of unknown battery drain by reporting kernel wake locks and partial wake locks. It has a steep learning curve, but once you figure out how to use it (start by Googling), you will be glad you did. Of course, if you're using Greenify, you should rarely need BetterBatteryStats.

WiFi Tether Router: In the past, many custom ROMs came with the TrevE WiFi package installed, but that app has not been updated in some time and does not work on many newer KitKat devices. WiFi Tether Router, available on the Google Play Store, allows you to tether your device's cellular connection without counting against your hotspot plan. In fact, you can even tether without paying for a hotspot plan at all. Of course, you should be aware that this might violate the terms of your contract.

Tasker: Tasker is a unique and super-powerful app. It lets you program your Android to do complex tasks in the background without your intervention. For example, you can have your Android start playing music any time it connects to your car's Bluetooth stereo, or disable the lock screen anytime you're on your home Wi-Fi network. The learning curve is even steeper than that of BetterBatteryStats, but the time investment is well worth it. To speedup the process, use Google to find Tasker tutorials.

Xposed Framework: Many root apps come in the form of Xposed plugins rather than standalone apps. You will need the Xposed Framework installed to take advantage of these plugins. I suggest installing it immediately after rooting if your custom ROM does not already include it.

Chapter 10: Accessory Shopping Guide

There is a wide range of accessories available for the Galaxy S5. In this chapter, I provide examples of both official and third party accessories to give you an idea of what is available. I also recommend specific accessories that I have experience with.

Please note that there are hundreds, if not thousands of accessories already available for the Galaxy S5, and it would be impossible to cover them all here. If you're interested in any of the accessories I discuss in this chapter, you should do your own research to compare prices and brands. For example, many of the official Samsung accessories I discuss have off-brand alternatives that may be just as good and/or cheaper. And, the products I link to may be cheaper from other vendors. This chapter is only a starting point.

If you register your Galaxy S5 on Samsung's website you will receive a coupon good for 50% off any mobile accessory.

http://www.samsung.com/us/support/register/product

After registering your Galaxy S5, you'll receive an email entitled "Your gift for registering your Galaxy S5," containing your coupon code for the Samsung store, linked below.

http://www.samsung.com/us/mobile/cell-phones-accessories

Cases

There are several categories of cases for the Galaxy S5. Personally, I use the inexpensive Cimo TPU cover ($10).

http://www.amazon.com/dp/B00IICJXDM

It protects the back and sides of the Galaxy S5. TPU cases are soft but firm plastic, and their biggest advantage is that they hold their shape very well and resist stretching over time. I like the Cimo case in particular because it has textured sides that provide a firm grip on the Galaxy S5. Similar TPU cases are available from most carriers' retail stores, although you'll likely pay 2-3 times what you would pay for a brand like Cimo online.

Sometimes, you can find cases like the Cimo but made of hard plastic. These are common on eBay, and usually sell directly from Asia for 3-4 dollars. However, I recommend TPU instead because of its texture and because it won't crack.

Another alternative is the Samsung S-View Flip Cover ($35), which provides more functionality but less protection. It flips open and closed, and while closed, the Galaxy S5 can display information such as the time and date through the window of the case.

http://www.amazon.com/dp/B00ITI22OC/

If you want something heavier-duty, the OtterBox Defender ($45) is a great solution. It provides excellent protection including a built-in screen protector, but will substantially increase your Galaxy S5's footprint.

http://www.amazon.com/dp/B00IPGVZWS

Other types of cases are available but less common, such as belt holsters, pouches, kickstand cases, and even wooden cases. Amazon and eBay are good starting points to find something more unusual.

Styli

Unlike the Galaxy Note series, the Galaxy S5 doesn't have a Wacom digitizer to support S Pen input. However, you can still purchase regular capacitive styli that have finer tips than the tip of your finger. You won't get nearly the same precision as with a Galaxy Note, but styli can still come in handy.

My favorite capacitive stylus is the Samsung C-Pen. It is made of sleek brushed metal, and has a finer tip than most similar units. However, it is also relatively expensive at a $25 street price.

http://www.amazon.com/dp/B0089VO7HY/

If you want a cheaper alternative, any product called a "capacitive stylus" will work. You can find cheap versions for as little as $3-4.

Cables & Connectivity

A number of data and video cables are available for the Galaxy S5, as well as some multi-function docks and other compatible accessories.

Audio/Video Connectivity

- An MHL 2.0 to HDMI adapter ($12.99) is the simplest and cheapest way to output your Galaxy S5's screen to an HDMI-enabled television or monitor.

http://www.amazon.com/dp/B00ESM3Q7K/

- Alternatively, you can opt for Samsung's AllShare Cast Wireless Hub ($50), which allows you to stream a variety of multimedia over Wi-Fi to your HDMI television or monitor.

http://www.amazon.com/dp/B0089VO7MY/

- If you're mainly concerned about streaming Netflix and YouTube video, you can also consider purchasing a Google Chromecast for use with your Galaxy S5. It doesn't support all of the Samsung-specific features of the AllShare Cast Wireless Hub, but it works great for streaming popular video services and costs less.

http://www.amazon.com/dp/B00DR0PDNE

> If you do buy a Chromecast, make sure to pick up a copy of my book, *Unlock the Power of Your Chromecast!*
>
> http://www.amazon.com/dp/1494820609

Data Cables

The Galaxy S5 has a Micro USB 3 port. If you're like me, you had probably never seen one of these until the last year or two. The first thing to know about Micro USB 3 is that it is fully compatible with Micro USB—you just need to be careful about where you jam the cable.

See the connector on the left? That's the same shape as the old Micro USB cables, and you can plug one into the Galaxy S5 if it's all you have with you.

The second thing to know is that using a Micro USB 3 cable is preferable when possible, as data transfer is faster assuming the connected device also supports USB 3.0. If you need an extra or a replacement, Amazon sells them for $5.99.

> **http://www.amazon.com/dp/B008EQZ25K/**

Also, consider picking up an inexpensive USB OTG cable to connect your Galaxy S5 to flash drives, mice, keyboards, and more ($1.47).

> **http://www.amazon.com/dp/B005QX7KYU/**

Read more about USB OTG here (p. 269).

SD Cards

The Galaxy S5 is compatible with Class 6 and 10 Micro SD memory cards of both the SDHC and SDXC variety. The maximum size supported is 128 GB.

> SDXC cards are no faster than SDHC cards; they simply support greater storage capacities. SDHC cards go up to 32 GB, so unless you need a 64 GB or larger card, SDHC is fine.

I use SanDisk Ultra cards, which are available at very reasonable prices through Amazon. Here is an affordable 32GB card:

http://www.amazon.com/dp/B009QZH7BU/

Headsets

The Galaxy S5 supports both wired and Bluetooth wireless headsets. (Most carriers include a basic wired headset in the box.) Samsung sells a variety of both, although Amazon has a larger selection and lower prices. Learn how to pair a Bluetooth headset <u>here</u> (p. 198).

Batteries & Chargers

The Galaxy S5 is a very power-hungry device, yet at the same time its battery life is considerable. To accomplish this, the Galaxy S5 uses a 2,800-mAh battery charged by a 2.0 amp charger. The Galaxy S5's charger is much more powerful than typical smartphone chargers, and is certainly outputs more current than any computer's USB port. For optimal charging times, you should always charge with the provided charger or a 2.0 amp equivalent, coupled with a Micro USB 3 cable.

Samsung sells several power accessories including standard spare batteries and a spare battery charging system. Note that the spare battery charging system ($49.99) is only $20 more than a spare battery alone ($29.99), and actually includes a spare battery in the package—so you're only paying $20 for the charger! You can also buy a wireless charging pad and cover that are compatible with the Qi wireless charging standard. All of these products can be found on Samsung's online store:

http://www.samsung.com/us/mobile/cell-phones-accessories/

You can use a non-Samsung Qi charging pad if you wish, but make sure it is compatible with the Galaxy S5's 2.0 amp requirement for the fastest charging time.

WARNING: Although the wireless charging products are convenient, they are slower than wired chargers. Additionally, the wireless charging cover is slightly thicker than the regular cover, and may be incompatible with some cases. I suggest carefully researching the combination of products you want before you spend your money.

Several third-party companies have also begun selling high-capacity batteries, which come with thicker covers and will affect case compatibility much like Samsung's wireless charging cover. You can find these on Amazon and eBay.

You can also buy rechargeable 9,000 mAh battery packs such as this one:

http://www.samsung.com/us/mobile/cell-phones-accessories/EEB-EI1CBAGSTA

(Short URL: http://goo.gl/5ENjPX)

If you look at other models, make sure they support at least 2.0-amp output for the fastest charging time for your Galaxy S5.

Also available are car chargers, and again, make sure to purchase a unit with a high enough current output such as this one:

http://www.amazon.com/dp/B00EE4A9SQ/

Screen Protectors

There are countless brands of screen protectors, some of which are only a couple dollars or less per pack. However, I suggest purchasing quality screen protectors for the Galaxy S5 to ensure optimal visual quality and fingerprint sensor functionality.

I have been a long time user of Spigen screen protectors, and recommend them wholeheartedly. The cheaper PET film version is quite good and is a much better value than the more expensive tempered glass version.

> **http://www.amazon.com/dp/B00I3ULLJS/**

Vehicle Docks

Samsung sells a Universal Vehicle Navigation Mount for the Galaxy series, which is compatible with the Galaxy S5. It is useful both for improving hands-free access, as well as if you plan to use your Galaxy S5 as your main GPS.

> **http://www.amazon.com/dp/B0089VO7HE/**

Another popular and cheaper option is the iOttie dashboard mount:

> **http://www.amazon.com/dp/B007FH716W/**

Other Accessories

Other accessories for the Galaxy S5 include, but are not limited to:

- **NFC TecTiles**: These are programmable RFID stickers. You can place them around your home, car, and office, and execute custom actions when you tap your Galaxy S5 against them. The Galaxy S5 is only compatible with TecTiles 2. Read more about TecTiles here (p. 268).

- **Smartwatches**: The Samsung Galaxy Gear 2 works as a companion device via Bluetooth, showing notifications and allowing control over features such as media and calls. The Galaxy S5 is also compatible with the Pebble line of smartwatches.

- **Various Other Peripherals**: Bluetooth keyboards, etc.

Mailing List

To thank you for purchasing *Samsung Galaxy S5: The 100% Unofficial User Guide*, I would like to offer you the chance to receive FREE updates to this book in your email inbox. Please take a minute to sign up:

http://www.aaronhalbert.com/phplist/?p=subscribe&id=4

(Short URL: http://goo.gl/qeqlDv)

My Other Books

If you enjoyed this book, you might be interested in purchasing one of my other books.

Samsung Galaxy Note 3: The 100% Unofficial User Guide

http://www.amazon.com/dp /1494832631/

Unlock the Power of Your Chromecast

http://www.amazon.com/dp /1494820609/

Total Bitcoin Security: How to Create a Secure Bitcoin Wallet Step-by-Step

http://www.amazon.com/dp /1494976803/